Psychic phenomena, prophetic dreams, lost gloves, and found avocados. Join Valerie on her raucous personal journey toward greater self-knowledge, happiness, and empowerment. Be inspired to commence your own sojourn and grow your intuition, wisdom, and joy.

KUDOS for *Brilliance Brewing*

"Valerie's books are one of a kind – precious and rare. She brings an incredible wit to life's spiritual journey that makes one's own ride a little smoother. Her ability to encompass all aspects of life with such grace and humor is astonishing to me. She has a rare gift of combining a brilliant writing style with superb humor. Truly a remarkable example of genius, in my humble opinion. Enjoy the ride! Namaste." ~ Nicole Gans Singer, Channeler, Teachings of the Masters, teachingsofthemasters.org

"With her ability to see the hidden meanings, and the humor, in everyday events from illness to "passport malfunction," the author takes us on an exhilarating journey that is both hilarious and through-provoking. A real gem of a read." ~ Taylor Jones, The Review Team of Taylor Jones & Regan Murphy

"Told in Gilbert's unique and refreshing voice and filled with thought-provoking ideas, I found the book to be both enjoyable and stimulating. Whether you are looking for wisdom and ways to improve your own life, or you just want to laugh and have your spirits lifted, *Brewing Brilliance* does both with ease. Keep it on your shelf to read again and again whenever you're feeling down." ~ Regan Murphy, The Review Team of Taylor Jones & Regan Murphy

ACKNOWLEDGMENTS

With gratitude to Editor Lauri Wellington and Black Opal Books for continuing to shine a light on my work. To Faith, Jack, Arwen, and LP at Black Opal, and to my Canadian friends, Lauren Tatner, Eniko Tolnai, and Mathew Hart. Special thanks to Courtney Valente (cvalente@cohoes.org) cover shot photographer, sunset on the Mohawk River, Latham, New York.

Also by Valerie Gilbert

Raving Violet

*Memories, Dreams and Deflections:
My Odyssey Through Emotional Indigestion*

Swami Soup

BRILLIANCE BREWING

A MEDITATION ON CHANGE

VALERIE GILBERT

A Black Opal Books Publication

GENRE: NON-FICTION/SELF-HELP/HUMOR

This book is a work of non-fiction. All information and opinions expressed herein are the views of the author. This publication is intended to provide accurate and authoritative information concerning the subject matter covered and is for informational purposes only. Neither the author nor the publisher is attempting to provide legal advice of any kind. All trademarks, service marks, registered trademarks, and registered service marks are the property of their respective owners and if used herein are for identification purposes only. The publisher does not have any control over or assume any responsibility for author or third-party websites or their contents.

BRILLIANCE BREWING
Copyright © 2017 by Valerie Gilbert
Cover Design by Jackson Cover Designs/Valerie Gilbert
Cover photograph: Courtney Valente
All cover art copyright © 2017
All Rights Reserved
Print ISBN: 978-1-626947-21-4

First Publication: AUGUST 2017

All rights reserved under the International and Pan-American Copyright Conventions. No part of this book may be reproduced or transmitted in any form or by any means, electronic or mechanical, including photocopying, recording, or by any information storage and retrieval system, without permission in writing from the publisher.

WARNING: The unauthorized reproduction or distribution of this copyrighted work is illegal. Criminal copyright infringement, including infringement without monetary gain, is investigated by the FBI and is punishable by up to 5 years in federal prison and a fine of $250,000. Anyone pirating our ebooks will be prosecuted to the fullest extent of the law and may be liable for each individual download resulting therefrom.

ABOUT THE PRINT VERSION: If you purchased a print version of this book without a cover, you should be aware that the book is stolen property. It was reported as "unsold and destroyed" to the publisher, and neither the author nor the publisher has received any payment for this "stripped book."

IF YOU FIND AN EBOOK OR PRINT VERSION OF THIS BOOK BEING SOLD OR SHARED ILLEGALLY, PLEASE REPORT IT TO: lpn@blackopalbooks.com

Published by Black Opal Books **http://www.blackopalbooks.com**

DEDICATION

*To the Brilliance within us all,
just waiting to be tapped.*

Table of Contents

Chapter 1
A Day In The Life

Chapter 2
Señor de los Milagros
(or Why Everyone was Shorter than Me)

Chapter 3
The Lights Are On and the Motor's Running, Part 1

Chapter 4
The Lights are On and the Motor is Running, Part 2

Chapter 5
Burn

Chapter 6
The Puppy Song

Chapter 7
On Being Happy

Chapter 8
Building Peace

Chapter 9
Avocado Dude

Chapter 10
The Mystical Bike Shop (An Interlude)

Chapter 11
Heaven's Gate

Chapter 12
Funeral For A Friend

Chapter 13
On A Clear Day You Can See Forever

Chapter 14
Food, Intuition, and Healing

Chapter 15
Meditation For People Who Don't Want To Meditate

Chapter 16
GOING DEEP: Mining the Gold Within

Chapter 17
BEGINNINGS: Or The Land of the Purple Glove

AFTERWORD
(More Signs, Symbols and Sigils!)

CHAPTER 1

A Day in the Life

I am a "weird" magnet. This kind of weird can only be attracted in New York, a vortex of concentrated human eccentricity. Contemplate my odd assortment of vignettes as an ambling film sequence.

Scene One, Take One: Returning home from tap class, I stop into my local wine shop, which I recently remembered used to be the neighborhood bakery when I grew up here. It's still my treat corner since fourth grade.

As I left, a very attractive man was standing in the sun against one of the buildings, about thirty feet away. Someone I know and have avoided since the passing of my beloved dachshund Mimi almost nine months ago. He's a silver fox from Mexico, gorgeous, gay, and a dog walker. He used to be particularly attached to my dog, even though no one ever walked her but me. He would see her and light up, as many people did, since she was such a supremely loving creature.

"I *love* you!" he'd gush to her with his accent as he scooped her up in his arms, cuddling her to his face and rocking with her in bliss, eyes closed, while other leashes and dogs radiated out from him like a maypole.

He saw me as I walked up the street, and I smiled at him. He mouthed and mimed as I approached, "Where is she?"

I shook my head soberly as I walked closer. His smile diminished as he awaited my explanation.

"She's gone," I said as I stood in front of him.

He was speechless.

Now, I've had some pretty hideous reactions upon informing people of Mimi's passing. "You're killing me!" screeched a morbid neighbor, a dog-owning widow with black shellacked hair and huge black sunglasses (reminiscent of Jackie O.) who allegedly poisoned her husband. Perhaps she was recalling her spouse's final words? She offered not one word of comfort to me. Somehow, this was all about her.

One day, a fellow doxie owner approached, and I decided not to dodge her and her giant longhaired dachshund, who my baby used to french kiss. The two dogs were a love match, although it was clear Luigi was seeing other women. Norma adored my dog, joyously exclaiming as vociferously as my girl, who squealed in delight and flopped on her back, tail wagging, upon seeing the tiny old lady and her big dog. Mimi engaged in this super friendly behavior often.

My senior neighbor Shirley, who refused to touch her, but clearly delighted in her from afar, called her a slut.

Shirley screamed when I told her Mimi had died. "But I never let her into my apartment!"

No, she hadn't. She missed out on having her home sniffed and searched by a very low, loopy dog who hopped and skipped due to her deformities.

Back to Norma. I thought Norma, who reveled in all things Mimi, would be devastated when I told her about Mimi's passing. I sobbed as I choked out the sad tale.

Norma was unmoved and said simply that I had to get another dog.

The next time I saw her was months later, and I was ready for her. I was better, less frail.

"Where's the puppy?" she said.

Norma's old, and I thought she was losing it. I sighed, patiently. "She passed, Norma."

"I know," she retorted. "Where's the *new* puppy?" Not senile. Pushy.

"I'm not getting a new puppy, Norma," I said quietly.

"Why not?" she barked.

"Because I'm not ready."

"Why not?" she barked again.

"Because I don't want another dog. I'm not ready" I defended.

"Why aren't you ready?" she needled.

"I'm just not. I want other changes in my life, not another dog," I tried to explain, but she persisted in pressing her dog dictate.

"Well, you can have other things and a dog, too. You're just stubborn, that's what you are!"

Suddenly, this, heretofore, cute little old lady I adored had become my prosecutor, while the Black Widow (who still has her dog) had acted as if my loss had been hers. That's why I don't talk about it.

But my Mexican friend, the silver fox standing in the sun, just looked and listened earnestly as I told the tale. "She became paralyzed, and I couldn't put her through surgery with all her other health issues. I know you loved her."

As I teared up, he reached into his pocket for a soft, neatly folded white paper towel, obviously a backup maintenance tool for his line of work. I demurred, used to wiping my fairly frequent tears on a sleeve. But he insisted and put it in my hand. I dabbed the folded rectangle to my eyes and continued. "I haven't been able to talk about it. She was only five, and she meant the world to me. It's just too sad."

Sergio did the kindest thing a person can do when one is distraught. He offered no comfort (beyond the "quicker picker upper") and no counsel. He just listened, beholding me while absorbing my story, a witness to my pain. It was the purest expression of love. Hugging him, I offered, "She loved you."

He looked me in the eye and blurted, "Be careful," his Mexican attempt at saying "take care," I suppose. As I walked away he blurted, "I love you," just like he used to say to my little baby.

"I love you, too." I said.

Since I was now all weepy and in need of succor, I clutched my just purchased chilled sauvignon blanc and headed over to my old stomping ground, the Catholic Church across the street. No, I don't drink in the pews. While not Catholic, I like the sanctuary to contemplate and regroup. Before Mimi, I used to sit there and weep when my mother was dying. With Mimi, I'd sneak her in in her bag, and we'd bask in the chill air on blisteringly hot days, or thaw and re-heat on the freezing cold ones. It is a modern church and usually quite empty, which is just the way I like it, a respite from the noisy world outside.

On this day it wasn't empty at all. There was no mass in progress, but a dispersed and disparate "crowd" of six were praying in earnest. I could feel the energy of their prayers, providing a very *Wings of Desire* film set atmosphere.

A white woman to my right in corduroy jeans knelt in front of a statue. A white woman to my left kneeled in front of St. Francis (a personal favorite of mine). A black woman in a powder blue suit and hat sat in front of me. A black man was to the left—human chess pieces spread out on an invisible Catholic game board.

The black lady in the blue suit started waving her right hand before her face, silently "testifying." This went on for a while and I took in the spectacle, one I'd never seen at this church, concluding that she was conversing with Jesus. She dropped her hand briefly but waved it again for a stretch. To my far left was a very old, tall white priest who always sits in the same chair. He's friendly but quiet and has a bum foot, his bones and bunions exploding out of his dirty, black, Velcro-trussed sneakers. His eyes were fixed on the bible in his lap, the same book he's read over and over for decades. Doesn't that tome get old after a while?

An attractive young Asian business woman was in church only to text, eyes glued to her glowing appliance in the back pew. Her phone rang. This was a first for me, and I was appalled that she'd add insult to injury by making noise on top of being so "textfully" disrespectful in this sacred space. She left the main area to turn it off, I supposed, but wouldn't you just know it? She took the freaking call in the outer hall, which we could clearly hear. I departed, leaving the *Six Characters In Search Of An Author* behind.

Speaking of crass, I ventured boldly into an institution I'd spent my entire life near, but had never entered. Central Synagogue is the oldest synagogue in New York City, established in 1846, with the building dedicated in 1872. While I venture freely into churches because they have open doors and people coming in and out, I had never done so in a synagogue because they seemed formidable versus accessible.

But a young lady in business attire climbed the steps toward the entrance, which made me think it was open. In all my life it had never seemed open or active. The building was a mysterious, impenetrable fortress. I seized the opportunity.

On my way to physical therapy, I was wearing shorts, sneakers, and a tee-shirt. Now, I know God doesn't mind about that kind of stuff 'cause God Is Everything, however, the people who run the synagogue might mind. That person that day was a big guy in a beige suit. He looked a bit like a Jewish bouncer. Given how *he* was dressed, I thought he might give me some tsuris for my getup (yes, *I* was the crass one in "church" this time). The pretty Israeli (I knew where she was from because she had an accent) business gal kept him busy with questions while I slipped in and sat. I explored the right to left, back to front, reading material in my Jewish pew and took in the décor. It looked just like a church. Throw in a Jesus here and a couple of crosses there, and you could house a whole other crowd.

Now, the physical therapy. I have a new insurance plan. I was very excited about this new insurance plan until I started using it. Don't get me wrong. I'm grateful for it. My audio book work through my union entitled me to pay for the privilege of having this insurance. I was thrilled to find out that they covered chiropractic and acupuncture, both of which I rely on. I'm an alternative therapies type and don't count on MDs for my well-being. I prefer preventative, holistic care and use MDs on an "as needed" basis only.

In the midst of enjoying my chiropractic and acupuncture benefits, I discovered that I was entitled to only half the number of treatments I thought I was. A real pity, for the healthier I am, the less actual *medical* treatment I need (the old "ounce of prevention is worth a pound of cure" thing). Getting weekly acupuncture and chiropractic was putting me in fine form and spirits. But I was also entitled to four physical therapy treatments, so I decided to cash in on that benefit, since I had wrist pain from my audio recording and editing work (I record, engineer and master the work myself) and knee pain from an old biking injury.

I needed a referral for physical therapy, so I selected the general practitioner closest to me, which wasn't all that close. But she was a girl, which I wanted, and had a cushy address just opposite the exclusive Tavern On The Green restaurant in Central Park. And she could take me immediately, so I could start my physical therapy immediately, with only a month left to this insurance quarter to cash in on those four sessions. Strangely, she was open for walk-in appointments only. I was advised there usually wasn't a long wait, and appointments lasted for only about twenty minutes.

Her office was on the main floor of a classic Central Park West building. The front door was on the sidewalk. I crossed the threshold and was suddenly starring in *The Wizard of Oz* in reverse. All the Technicolor drained from my day as I entered her desiccated den from another time period altogether—somewhere between the 1940s and the 1960s. This joint was untouched by time, money, renovations, or a cleaning crew. Everything was brown. The miniscule bathroom, which I needed to use, abutted the sidewalk. The toilet was right by the old thin window so I could hear loud footsteps on the street inches away from me as I sat exposed, pants down. My need to relieve myself vanished. I saddled up and went to the sink, which looked distinctly…unclean. I've seen tidier bathrooms in fast food restaurants. What kind of a doctor's office was this?

The shop was run by three older women. A black woman was so large it proved difficult for her to get out of her chair. She remained seated against the wall in the anteroom for the duration of my visit. A petite Latina woman was friendly, efficient, and ran the desk and phone. When I'd asked if the doctor was nice, she responded that she'd been with the doctor for thirty years. And then there was the old battle-axe herself, a white gal who'd graduated from medical school in 1943. Now, I knew that little tidbit going in. The insurance site listed her stats. But I was not prepared for the full *Grey Gardens* effect generated by the doctor and her medical practice.

A ninety year-old former show-girl stood before me. The good doctor was rail thin, sporting bright red lipstick and long blonde hair coiffed to Barbie Doll perfection. Her breasts were reminiscent of Carol Burnett's costume when she played "Charro's Mother" since they were thin, long, low, and—it seemed—irregular. Her colorful polyester shirt and pencil skirt were a throwback to the 1970s (when they were undoubtedly purchased). She wore her purse around her neck hanging in front of her stomach, like the sporrans that Highland Scotsmen don over the front of their kilt. Her rectangular shoulder bag hung from a long, thin gold chain and was as thin and two dimensional as she was. The edges were totally frayed, and I could not tell whether it was made of decomposing black-patent-leather-faux "alligator" or authentic cardboard and plastic. In addition to assorted jewelry, her final accessory was a vintage stethoscope. My face registered the same shock exhibited in the countenances of the Broadway audience in Mel Brooks's 1968 masterpiece, *The Producers*, upon realizing that they were watching a musical homage to Hitler.

I was frozen in an episode of *The Twilight Zone*, a David Lynch film, or *The Cabinet of Dr. Caligari*. Take your pick. I was on set.

I signed a few forms, my uneasy smile trying to mask my mortification. What would happen to me in this medical house of horrors? There were piles of paper everywhere, on top of army-green metal filing cabinets and index card-holders from the '40s, '50s, and '60s. Labels were hand scrawled "Medicaid" and "Medicare." There was no computer visible anywhere, but a fax machine collected dust. My eyes scanned the joint from top to bottom. It was a museum exhibit. A total time warp to the 1960s New York City of my childhood.

"The doctor will see you now."

The receptionist jarred me out of my reverie. I entered the examining room. The medical equipment was from the 1930s and 1940s, including a vintage baby scale and examination table. *Young Frankenstein's* lab now came to mind. The antediluvian table had stirrups for gynecological use, and musty mechanical cranks beneath. Scalpels, tweezers, and antiquated metal tools were scattered about, mixed in with piles of rubber bands, vaccines, needles, and pens. More file cabinets were piled haphazardly on top of each other.

"What's wrong with you?" blurted the old woman as she entered the room.

"Uh, nothing. I need a referral to see a physical therapist."

She sat down across from me on one of her mismatched chairs. "I told you to sit on the other chair, it's more comfortable," she directed me.

She'd said "sit on the *round* chair" so I'd sat on the round wooden stool. Apparently, she told me to "sit on the *brown* chair," which was cracked pleather and chrome.

The stool was white and the cleanest, newest thing in the room. I stayed put.

"Do you have any illnesses?"

"No," I replied.

"Family history?"

I gave her a brief rundown of how everyone died, including my mother's death from cancer.

She took laborious longhand notes on an oversized index card, then looked up at me abruptly, "Breast cancer?"

"No," I replied.

She didn't bother to find out what kind of cancer my mother actually had. She asked me my weight and height without bothering to verify my claims. I grew a couple inches and lost a couple pounds. If she was living in a dream world, then so could I.

Dr. Norma Desmond instructed me to me hop up on the edge of the gruesome examining table. If ever a piece of equipment was haunted, this was it. I could feel the fear from myriad patients emanating from the frayed pad and rusted chrome. She listened to my heart with her trusty stethoscope. She felt my left breast then got distracted when I told her I had fibroid tumors in my uterus. She briefly palpated my lower abdomen and made no comment. So much for my right breast.

She looked in my ears with her ear-thingie then tried to get her flashlight to turn on so she could look down my throat. She fiddled with it, but it didn't work, so she banged it hard on the stirrup. Bam. It was on.

That over, we discussed my wrist pain, the very reason I was there. She placed my wrist on the stirrup. I kid you not. Maybe this contraption did double duty back in the day, but to me, now, it was a gynecological stirrup, and my wrist was on it. Jeremy Irons in *Dead Ringers* leered at me from the side of the room.

She asked if I wanted blood work, and had she been a real doctor, I would have accepted the offer. But not trusting her to hit a forearm let alone a vein, I declined. Perhaps this was where the large black woman came in. It's possible that she was a nurse. But drawing my blood would necessitate her getting up, and this seemed unlikely.

Norma Desmond hand scrawled my referral for the physical therapy, said "Anything else?" then suggested I take two more referrals, one for a gynecologist and another for an orthopedist. *This*, then, was her specialty. Penning referrals.

Relieved to be done, I was shocked to find other people in the waiting room. All women. All older. What were they doing here? What did this doctor do all day? Right. She handed out referrals. It was clear that neither she nor her staff were in any condition to treat anyone for anything.

I approached the front desk with $20 for my $10 copay. "Doctor," her receptionist ventured, it seemed to me with trepidation. "Do you have $10 change for this lady's co-pay?"

Here was the purpose of the shiny, dilapidated purse swinging from doc's neck. It was the bank. She didn't trust her employee of thirty years to hold the $10s? Well, just add that to the pile of crazy.

As I exited the joint, I walked to nearby Sheep's Meadow on this glorious May day to regroup and slowly adjust to 2014. An iced coffee from Tavern on the Green's pleasant take-out window aided in my recovery, and a Garage Band workshop at the Apple store on Fifth Avenue completed my reentry into today's space-time coordinates.

The camera cuts to me, medium shot, walking the streets the next day wearing shorts, tee shirt, and sneakers, clutching my hard-won physical therapy referral as I exit Central Synagogue. From there I went directly to my new physical therapy practice in a very respectable office building, only to find that *this* operation had not been renovated since the early 1980s. This is not encouraging in a medical establishment. One wants the latest, the newest, and the best. I was having medical disappointment déjà vu.

Hoping for some nurturing medical massage as part of the package, all I saw were boring weights and machines. Looked like I'd have to do all the work. Sigh.

My therapist was a tall, no-nonsense gal, and her very basic equipment also seemed, well, quite old. She measured my wrist with a glorified tape measure from a plastic box of supplies that could have once housed a Lego set. The joint was uninspired. Even Norma Desmond had had some freaky flair.

I tried to crack a joke but my therapist was a tough customer. She alternately boiled and froze my wrist with very hot and very cold things then sono-waved it. She showed me a few stretches and the proper way to sit at my computer. Snore. This "therapy" basically boiled down to a lecture on posture.

While she was taking my carpal deposition, we sat inches away from each other, face to face in a little cubicle.

At one point she sighed. "You have to take better care of yourself."

I'd been working like a dog producing audio books day and night in my home studio, a distraction from the grief of losing my dog. I'd pushed myself to the point of pain and had traded sentimental grief for physical maladies.

Tears started rolling down my face.

This threw her totally off her game when she looked up from my wrist. She was offering "*physical*" therapy, not "*therapy*" therapy. She tossed some rough paper towels at me so I could clean up my emotional mess, but not compassionately the way Sergio the dog walker had gently offered his soft towel to me. Her turf was repairing tendons and muscles, not the tender buttons she was pressing. But I needed nurturing, not needling.

That being said, she gave me some good advice about posture, and her seminal "You have to take better care of yourself" had struck a nerve.

I thought I already was doing that. But there's always farther to go.

Taking better care of yourself emotionally, financially, physically, spiritually, and mentally, the whole shebang, is what it's all about. Loving yourself has many facets.

A day in my life combines smiling, celebrating, crying, napping, pontificating, dancing, cooking, eating well, biking, blading, solitude, more solitude, writing, and recording. Day by day, gently (and sometimes more forcefully), I edge toward beautiful new vistas where grief abates and happiness abides. Sunset. Music swells. Fade to black.

CHAPTER 2

Señor de los Milagros
(Or Why Everyone Was Shorter Than Me)

I love signs from Spirit. I live by them. Dreams and visions inform my days and nights. They leave a trail of breadcrumbs for me to follow, and sometimes, an entire organic, whole grain loaf fresh from the oven to enjoy.

There are many ways that Spirit communicates with us, and, when I say Spirit, I mean God, your Higher Self, your True Self, or your angels, guides, and loved ones in spirit, who are with you always. It doesn't matter how you perceive the invisible realms. There is help and support available at all times, and I use it.

A hermit in midtown Manhattan, I work at home and live alone. It's been this way for quite a while, all the more so since my last two pets, a dog and cat, died twelve and eighteen months ago, respectively. I was too upset to get more animals, and determined that I'd spring for a human the next time. I'm due a relationship.

However, Spirit has other ideas about this. They've been keeping me in quarantine, with an etheric chastity belt to boot. They keep telling me there's more work to do before my long awaited partnership happens. This does not make me happy, for I am human and have longings for company and intimacy. However, I also believe my soul charted this path, and that I'm not an unwitting player. I understand and embrace the agenda, yet still get frustrated from time to time. For the most part, I'm pretty damn happy with my life right now. I've learned to raise and keep my vibration at a consistently high level. Whatever momentarily glitches get my knickers in a twist, I'm able to recover from with relative ease and bounce back quickly. Weebles wobble, but they don't fall down.

Apparently, solitude has been essential for my spiritual incubation, the fertile soil I've needed to process my grief, angst, and what have you. Stuff. I'm very human while yet a decidedly fervent mystic. Embracing the seeming paradox of the human and divine worlds is the basis of my credo. This world is full of contradictions, being a world of duality. We must conceive *beyond* limitation. To transcend duality into triality, the point above the fray, and strive to attain the eagle's eye vista.

I was told (by Spirit) that more spiritual and creative doors have to open for and within me before I am mated. I must climb higher on the ladder of ascension, and that my most important mating is with my Higher Self. This is not the hot date I'm looking for on a Friday night. I'm the only bride I know required to wear a freaking halo on her head for her wedding day. What kind of lace goes with *that*?

I will now discuss with you here how signs and symbols from Spirit work.

For instance, I've been dreaming of dumplings lately, on several occasions. Don't ask me why. Chinese dumplings, specifically. You know, dim sum? Steamed, pan fried, whatever. Dim sum dumplings. I make note of my dreams as they are insightful, potent, and often prophetic. For someone who regularly interprets her dreams, dumplings represent...an enigma. What the hell do dumplings mean? Beats me. But I wrote it down anyway. I record my dreams every day. There were at least three separate dream dumpling incidents over the course of six weeks. Mystifying, in a very doughy way.

Well, recently, I had a breakdown. Not new. I break down all the time. And that does not mean that I am broken. It means that I am sensitive, and in touch with my feelings. I don't put on a happy face when I ain't happy. In fact, I read recently that babies (very in touch with the "other side" from which they have freshly emerged) will often cry not because something is wrong with them, but because something is *wrong*. Period. They pick up on the energetic malcontent on the planet. There's a lot of it. Are you surprised?

Perhaps I'm depressed, a sad sack, or a genius. Or perhaps, I too, like the babies, pick up on the pain on this planet. Or recall my own. From this lifetime and others. Who hasn't suffered? The Buddha nailed it. Life is suffering (from one perspective). From other perspectives, physical life is a joke, an illusion, a game to be conquered, a realm to be enjoyed, learned from, and, in so doing, we uplift ourselves to higher dimensions. Suffering is one perspective. It's not the only one. The Buddha transcended it. So can we.

I wake up at four a.m. these days, when I take my new thyroid medication, which I plan to quit pronto. I'll be letting my thyroid doc know when I see him shortly. I suspect he won't be pleased, but then, he's just my doctor. It's my body.

This imbalance is a new condition. When I first went to him, I was concerned that he'd want to medicate me, but Doc was content to just monitor me without treatment (to my delight) until he learned a few months later that I was having knee surgery, at which point he freaked out.

"You're having *surgery*? You're doing it backward! You should be balancing your thyroid first, *then* getting surgery."

Why surgery necessitated taking thyroid pills, I don't know. He didn't explain. He just huffed and puffed. But, as against meds as I am generally (I'm a vitamin girl), I went along with Doc and started the pills.

I had a bike accident six years ago and suffered a complex tear of the medial meniscus (torn cartilage in the middle of the knee), which has caused pain and uncomfortable crackling and crunching ever since. I've waited years for the right insurance, the right surgeon, and the right time to get the situation remedied. I wasn't putting the big event off for the rantings of some old endocrinologist.

When the day of the surgery arrived, the hospital gave me an epidural, lightweight crutches, a turkey sandwich, and cranberry juice. It was Thanksgiving come early, and I had a fantastic time.

They gave me two pain pills after I came to. "Is there happiness in here?" I queried skeptically, for I was already pretty darn happy.

"Yes, there is."

For a full twenty-four hours after surgery I was happy as a clam, thanks to their ministrations and medications.

Then I stopped taking the pain pills, and it all became clear to me. Surgery is pretty fun and all, but it's not *that* much fun. I was high as a kite for a day.

In fact, I had a medical dream team, from a top surgeon to a darling anesthesiologist who looked like Roger Sterling from *Mad Men*. "Hi, I'm your bartender," he coyly introduced himself.

Yes! A compadre. "Speaking of which," I said, "can

I drink tonight?" assuming I knew the depressing answer.
"Of course!" he replied.
I was shocked and thrilled.
"What are you having?" he asked.
"Wine." I returned.
"Red or white?"
"Well, it's still warm out (it was September) so I think I'll go with white."
"Good choice" he replied. I glanced over at the nurse to my right who was attempting to thread an IV into my wrist, a first for me. I'd heard that hurt a lot. "I'm trying to distract you with the bar talk," said the sly anesthesiologist.
"Thank you." I turned my attention away from the nurse with sharp things and back to the good-looking doctor who encouraged inebriation (to my relief the IV only hurt a little). I was careful to skip my happy pill with the prosecco at dinner.

Back to our regularly scheduled programming.

I have to take this thyroid pill first thing in the morning, thirty minutes before eating. After a brief meditation when I wake up, I like to eat (it's a happy way to start the day). Since I wake up in the middle of the night anyway, I decided that's when I'd take the pill so when I wake up in the morning, I don't have to wait around to get the food party started.

Waking at four a.m. of late, I'll get up and record audio books. Since I live in New York City and don't have a sound proof studio (which costs tens of thousands of dollars), I have to work around my sound constraints. It's relatively quiet at four and five in the morning. I get some prime recording done then edit later. But the recording sessions necessitate silence.

I'll have lunch between ten and eleven. Sometimes I have a glass of wine with my lunch. I look at myself askance as I glance at the clock, but then I do the math. It's not morning. It's lunchtime.

This one day I had an early lunch, replete with glass of wine, and, for whatever reason, I also had a nervous breakdown. Tears, loneliness, and frustration all welled up within me. I work. I exercise. I just had surgery. I meditate. I'm practically a perfect person, all things considered. I've survived death, death, and more death, of loved ones, human, feline, and canine. I'm all deathed out.

This glass of wine tipped me over the edge. While I believe marriage is in the cards for me (though in which deck, I don't know), I have no idea when it will happen.

In the past, while maudlin and tipsy, I'd look for love online. This time, I went to the website of an adoption center. They had a tiny little kitten featured called Dumpling. That was all I needed, a big fat neon sign from Spirit. I grabbed my wallet and identifying paperwork and, still crying, headed to the shelter in the pouring rain.

I cried on the way down to the shelter. I cried on the way back. The whole thing felt tainted, as cute as the kittens were. It felt like defeat. I didn't want to die a crazy cat lady, or "the single gal with the dog." So much for my holding out for a relationship.

I was regressing. A kitty recidivist. But better a stray cat than a stray man. I adopted two females. Now I could die happy with two cats, one dog (someday), and no husband, just like God intended. I'll probably get a freaking hippopotamus and a zebra, too. That's what I get for liking Saint Francis, patron saint of animals.

Apparently, other people had been dreaming of Dumpling, too. Because everyone was at the shelter to get her, although I was there first. A Russian girl and her husband felt Dumpling was destined for them because their other cat was named Taco. Like tacos and dumplings go together? They're totally mismatched cuisines. I relinquished Dumpling to a half-Asian, half-European, all-gay couple who took their little appetizer home in a snazzy purple carrier.

There was little Steven, white and ginger, who was sleeping in a car to keep warm when the driver started the engine. The kitten's leg got caught in the fan belt and the shelter had to amputate his leg. Even with three legs Steven was still the hyperactive terror of the kitty room. Always knock on the hood of your car to wake up sleeping animals if you park outside during winter.

Little black and white Eggplant seemed depressed, or sick. I asked the shelter's cat wrangler about this. Her siblings, Broccoli and Squash had been adopted the day before. Perhaps she was sad. I selected black and white "tuxedo" Eggplant and renamed her Marlena (after Dietrich, the original tuxedo wearer) and a tiny tiger tabby, Celeste.

Most gals get pregnant when they get drunk. I got kittens.

The sign from Spirit regarding Dumpling was crystal clear. While she was not my intended kitten, her name was the trigger, the call to action. That's how signs work. I was meant to have these two furry lunatics to soften my life. My initial trauma about yet again committing myself to the care and maintenance of two little rascals has since melted into a pool of purring. And I subsequently found out that dim sum literally translates into "Touch The Heart." Are my dreams cool, or what?

I had another powerful dream which mystified me at first (as is often the case until I've figured out the symbolism, or until the event it foretells unfolds). I saw a smallish fish tank (the size people keep in their homes) with a tiny (two to three feet) orca whale in it. The water was green/yellow, dark and murky, and the orca's skin was rotting and falling off of it. Kinda gross. However it ascended from the depths of the tank, rising to the surface. I knew it referred to some sort of resurrection, but whose?

I made the connection one day when I looked at tiny kitten Marlena, my first ever black and white "tuxedo" cat. It turned out she was very sickly when I adopted her. Remember, I said she seemed sad or sick when I was looking to adopt her and the shelter lady replied that it was probably because her littermates were adopted out the day before? Well, after adopting Marlena, it turned out she had worms (despite their having "de-wormed" her). This seriously nauseated me since I kissed the kittens, and I wished I were a hardcore whiskey drinker since humans can get them from their pets. I resorted to my default wine for my purge and supercharged it with my intentions to kill anything untoward.

I de-wormed both kittens again then took Marlena to my regular vet a few weeks later, who said, "She seems depressed."

She still had worms, it turned out. She was rail thin, bony, and wouldn't eat. I was worried about her survival. We gave her one last dose of de-worming medicine (each time with a dose to the other kitten, too, since it's always a tandem tainting, although Celeste was thriving).

While staring at Marlena, it occurred to me one day that her markings are very much like an orca's. Her chest, chin, and jaw are white, while the rest of her (save four white paws) is jet black. I understood my dream then and knew that Marlena would rise from the depths. And she did. She's now HUGE (not unlike a whale) at three feet long, nose to tail, tall and leggy (like her namesake, Dietrich).

And while she's still a very picky eater, and a very sensitive, soulful spirit, she's most certainly not underweight. She's dignified, quiet, and mysterious. Marlena is my Egyptian Temple Cat.

On to more magic and miracles.

I'm pals with a nun I met eight years ago at a new age retreat. She's a new age Catholic nun. While you wouldn't expect such a combination, there you have it. She's from Ireland and lives in Houston.

We share the same birthday (though she's older than me) and the same "out there" metaphysical taste. She sends me things from time to time, mostly books, sometimes inspirational decks, like the "Ascended Masters" oracle cards, and articles about health or spirituality.

Being hungry for mystical experience, she's been to healer John of God in Brazil, and Lourdes in France. Sister Eileen sent me a tiny plastic vial of their holy water, embedded in a color card of our Lady of Lourdes, sealed in plastic. I taped the whole thing to the wall by my desk. It stayed there a good year until I noticed the water table was dropping. Even in hermetically sealed plastic and shrink wrapped in yet more plastic, the holy water was evaporating somehow. Well, I didn't want it to disappear into the ethers without my partaking of its healing qualities. So, I broke it open, poured a drop or two on the crown of my head and swallowed the rest.

As there was yet a milliliter of holy water in it, I left the plastic tube on my desk. I'd let the magical residue evaporate.

Working at my desk a day or two later, I saw something move out of the corner of my eye. When I record audio books, it is of the utmost importance that *nothing* move, including me. I wear soft, silent clothing and keep my head steady. There are no stray sounds or rustling movements, just mouth to microphone. I'm a talking mime.

Puzzled by the movement on my desk, I stopped recording. The elliptical tube of plastic from Lourdes was rocking all by itself, as if someone had just tapped it. Except no one was there. I hadn't rocked my desk or knocked into anything—heck, you can't even raise an eyebrow without the sound picking up on the mic. Nothing else on my desk moved. Nothing anywhere moved. Just the tube that had held the holy water. It continued to rock for several seconds.

Who tipped the container with a flick of their spirit "finger"? Could be anyone. I don't see 'em. But I know they're there because it's not possible for something to "just happen by itself." There's always a reason or source, cause and effect. If it's not physical, then it's metaphysical. It's all energy anyway. Matter is just energy vibrating at a slower rate.

There's also no physical explanation for how the tiny wind chime I have hanging in my bathroom started swaying by itself. It's way above my head, to the right of my sink. If I want to ring it, I have to get up on tippy toes and nudge it with a fingertip. There's no window in my bathroom and therefore no wind. I was brushing my teeth. As clean as my teeth are, my brushing does not produce gusts. Even with an electric toothbrush, this was not a wind-generating event.

I saw or sensed something moving, and looked up. They didn't make a sound. But the chimes were swaying. As if someone had just gently touched them. My first thought is always, "How the heck did that happen?" I look around for the plausible, logical, physical explanation. When there isn't one, I say, "Hola!" to whoever is there interacting with me.

Then there was the time I heard sound coming from two rooms away. I continued working, late at night, but, when the sound continued for five minutes or so, I finally went out to investigate. My living room speaker had been turned on, and my iPod, in shuffle mode, had tuned itself to one of my favorite Pat Metheny songs, *Sueno Con Mexico*. Those who understand just say "cool!" (which is the proper response). Those that don't, why are you reading this? I'm all about this stuff, if you don't know by now, and I'm not letting up. I'm here to tell you, we're here to have fun with the unseen dimensions from whence we emerged—interacting, playing with, and breaching imperceptible walls.

My fourth tiny miracle was when I walked down Lexington Avenue in midtown lunch-hour foot traffic. It was a sunny September day, the street filled with people scurrying to and fro. A large bug flew at me. Not a common occurrence, I warily looked down to see what it was. A baby dragonfly (hello, this is *Manhattan*) flew right onto my heart. To boot, I was wearing a tee shirt with a big heart in the center. But this little animal totem flew directly to the left of my chest and parked. I didn't move. I pulled over to the side of the sidewalk, with the lunch crowd rushing past me. Right in front of Victoria's Secret, no less, with a bug perched on my boob. It stayed there a good five minutes. Gorgeous. Special. No mistaking the sign from Spirit. Dragonflies signify transformation (change, adaptability, joy, lightness of being). So, my heart was transforming. And, by the way? Victoria doesn't have a secret. It's called small underwear and big tits.

I've been going to a lot of spiritual events lately, the opposite of my hiding at home stunt that I did for the better part of a year after my dog Mimi died. I've finally got some spring in my step, and while I didn't leave the house before, now you can't keep me in. I've got ants in my pants. I went on a rampage, signing up for events, but one event in particular I was on the fence about. I just wasn't sure what was in it for me. So, I didn't pre-pay.

The morning of the event, I was exhausted, and relieved I hadn't bought a ticket. Ten minutes later, I was restless again, and decided to go.

I got a reading that morning from my friend Nicole Gans Singer, a terrific channeler, www.teachingsofthemasters.org. Her guides commented on my upcoming event that day, acknowledged that it was important that I go, and that I should meditate prior. The event was part of a big new age extravaganza, one I'm not partial to. It's a cheesy event in a cheesy hotel. If there was anything to turn a person off of new age stuff, this was it. And I'm new age. It's a carnival of crazy.

The speaker was someone whose work I greatly admire, however her ninety-minute event was a debacle of sorts. Her team, audio visual and otherwise, was disorganized. It was practically a joke. Fortunately, she got the joke and laughed. I like her. Despite that, on a conscious level I learned nothing, gleaned nothing, and was stuck with a bunch of weirdos, one of whom (right next to me, of course) *reeked* of garlic. The event seemed a waste of both my time and money. If I hadn't known Spirit was gunning for me to be there (they explained the energetic reason why I should go), I'd have felt disgusted. But I know better now. There's more to life than meets the eye. And I felt better not being at home. I left the carnival lickety-split and walked home from Herald Square. It was a sunny October day. I needed some exercise and some grounding, so I called my cousin while I walked home.

She's new age, too, and she understands crazy. She's dating a hoarder, a new relationship, and this habit of his is not to her liking, as she comes from a family with a tendency toward it. She helped him weed through his piles of stuff recently. "I asked him if I could throw something out. He didn't answer, so I pretended I heard him say 'yes' and got rid of it."

While we were talking on the phone, I made it to St. Patrick's Cathedral on Fifth Avenue where a huge mob had assembled. I thought it was a protest. Nope. Was the pope there? No. I edged in closer to the crowd. Everyone was taking pictures. From the center of the church's dark interior slowly emerged a heavy, purple religious float hoisted on the shoulders of many mocha-complected men. In fact, I was surrounded by people who were all darker than me. They were not, however, taller than me. And I'm not tall. This was a short, Latin American population.

Women, wearing lace scarves over their heads, swayed smoky silver incense holders in front of them, giving the pretzel, chestnut, and hot dog vendors aromatic competition. This was heavy duty ritual, and I was mesmerized. I studied the float. Jesus was suspended in his usual depressing pose. On the back, the Virgin Mary held baby Jesus, reminiscent of happier times. I got excited when I spotted a beautiful silver dove icon.

I finally asked someone what was going on.

An Australian tourist answered, "It's the Procession of the Miracles."

Huh? I'd never heard of that one, have you? You know why? It's a *Peruvian* ritual. The Catholic Church must be on hard times if they're hitting up South American countries for their customers and renting out Gothic St. Pat's for parties. No wonder I was the tallest person in sight save the Australian.

"Well, the miracle is going to be making it through this mob!" I replied.

"Yeah, and when you push through you're gonna' be a billionaire!" he quipped with his Aussie accent.

But I didn't want to push on just yet. I was caught up in the mystique of this ritual. I was still on the phone with my cousin, who was vicariously enjoying the proceedings. Bells clanged. Incense wafted as the procession continued through the packed crowd.

I blurted out, "Oh my God, there are live doves!"

A man clutched two white doves to his chest, preparing to release them. Remembering the last time the pope pulled that stunt (Weren't the doves immediately attacked and eaten by seagulls? Talk about a bad sign.), I was eager to see how these two would fare on Fifth Avenue. One flew up in the air to be met by a dark gray pigeon. Would it attack and kill? Nah, it probably just wanted a date. The other, freakishly, flew right back down into the crowd, near me.

People went crazy touching it, holding it, clutching it to their faces, taking photos with their families. I was concerned that this symbol of peace was being manhandled, albeit by eager and pious people. It didn't mean this dove wouldn't get crushed to death by their enthusiasm. I finally got hold of the dove, taking it gently from a *tiny* (three feet tall?) old woman in a black shawl who'd been monopolizing it. I let it stand in my hand. There would be no clutching and crushing on my watch. I wondered why it didn't fly. Was it hurt? It was covered in green bird crap, obviously from both birds being trapped and petrified prior to being released.

The old lady tried to grab it back from me but I barked, "No!"

I walked away from the crowd, toward the giant art deco statue of Atlas across from the church. There were planted flowers on a granite ledge in front of the statue. I put the dove on the stone shelf. It seemed dazed then meandered over the flowers. A guy near me offered to take it home, but I somehow didn't trust him. I wanted her to escape. When someone yet again attempted to grab her, she flew up, but only as far as the Banana Republic sign, clutching the metal letters in an incredibly awkward position, like she was holding on, sideways, for dear life. Why didn't she just fly away?

"Her foot's stuck!" someone shouted.

They jumped up to try to dislodge it, and, with that final assault, the dove flew up and away, into a tall tree. Finally! She then dove right back down into the crowds. Why would she fly back into the mayhem when she was free of it? Was there a dove shrink here somewhere? I didn't wait to see what happened to her next. I was done with my dove watch.

The Miracle Jesus float turned the corner, west up Fifty-First Street, along with his Peruvian entourage. Jesus's ripped and bloodied hands and feet don't look too different from mine, shredded and skewered by my new, tiny kittens.

Life.

There's blood, death, smoke, magic, and mystery at its very core.

CHAPTER 3

The Lights are on and the Motor's Running

Part 1
Warming Up The Engine

"Sucking or blowing?" I inquired. My doorman looked up at me, simultaneously confused, perturbed, and amused. *"What?"* he queried with his English accent.

I had returned home late at night after a screening of the amazing film *The Imitation Game* about British math genius Alan Turing, who broke the German code Enigma during WWII, and invented the world's first computer in so doing. The film stars Benedict Cumberbatch, who was there with the director and cast for a Q&A after the film, and then exited the theater to embrace his fiancée when all was said and done. I am a fan of Cumberbatch and his body of work, and this film *is* fantastic.

I was all misty after the film, not because I saw Benedict, nor because he is getting married (to someone else), but because my father fought in the war, and was stationed as an American airman in England. As well, it seems (this is relatively recent news) that my father may have been doing covert work for the government, and this film was all about "covert." I downgraded my crying from downpour to drizzle and wiped at my eyes as I approached my apartment building, shifting in mood from pensive and sad to puzzled and curious as I scrutinized my night doorman. I could not discern what he was doing outside the building. He was using a gadget on the sidewalk that looked like a leaf blower, but he then utilized it inside the lobby where, clearly, there were no leaves. Hence, my question. "Is it sucking, or blowing? I can't tell."

His bewilderment at my question gave way to laughter.

I go in spurts with my assorted activities, from tap dancing to spiritual seeking. I regularly get messages from Nicole Gans Singer, a childhood friend I haven't seen since sixth grade and lost touch with for decades. She's a medium and wonderful channeler. After being left high and dry time and again by the various and sundry "spiritual" events I attend, I've asked for feedback from Nicole's guides regarding some of these events, as there's often more (or less) than meets the eye. Maybe I did benefit from something, even if it seemed like a boring bust. It's all in one's perspective, and I like mine to be challenged. I keep an open mind, but am often flabbergasted by the unexpected insights Spirit has about my daily comings and goings.

I attended an event led by "energy worker" Abdy "Electriciteh" (a made up last name if ever I heard one). I'd heard about him from a Chatty Cathy in a trance mediumship class I once took, or "trance camp" as I liked to call it.

The girl gushed ecstatically, "Abdy looks in your eyes then knocks you down with his energy!"

Sounded like a barrel full of monkeys. There's a Croatian guy named Braco (pronounced "Bratzoh") who just stares warmly and intently at crowds for extended periods of time. It's supposed to be healing. Or loving. Or something. Anyone who's come close to their favorite movie or music star knows the electrifying phenomenon that Abdy was selling. What did people get from Jesus? The Buddha? What do they get from Bono? Heck, performance artist Marina Abramović made a splash at the Museum of Modern Art doing the same thing as Braco (though her energies are very dark in focus and intent. She is not a lightworker). A little eye contact goes a long way. It's increasingly rare in our mobile device obsessed culture. And charisma is always captivating. Comfortable eye contact, inner peace and social ease are antidotes for "text neck" and ADHD.

I was at another guy's channeling event in New York City when I learned that Abdy "Electriciteh" was going to be in New York City. Actually, I have to stop right there. I used to attend this fellow's channeled events regularly in years prior, and while all channeling sessions can be weird (it's awkward, on occasion, when another consciousness takes over your body), this guy's sessions were weirder than most.

I've been in dark, quiet rooms filled with reverent, meditative types when a channel's sudden booming voice made me hit the ceiling. In the weekly development circle I led in my home for years, a one-time guest channeled spontaneously, and I nearly jumped out of my skin. I didn't know she had that psychic trick up her sleeve. Actually, I didn't know if she was a girl, either, despite her overblown feminine façade. When you're over six feet tall and have no hips, big tits, big hair, and a lot of makeup become suspect.

I've been with soft-spoken channels, loud channels, and channels who babbled intergalactic gobbledeygook (hey, I don't speak Arcturian, it could have been coherent.) I'm open to it all. I don't have to prove it. It's not a test. It's an experience. I get what I get. And you get it from me. Some of it's real. Some of it may not be. But there's only one way to find out. Go to the group. Or go to Arcturus.

The guy whose channeled sessions I was going to weekly would gesticulate and spasm while he boomed. Weird? Yes. I could handle it. But years later, now that he's a big channeling star of sorts, all of a sudden his guides had taken on an English accent and a bit of Irish flair from time to time. The two accents phased in and out during his Big Free Public Appearance. This would seem flagrant proof that the fellow is faking, right? (You're barely with me as it is, I know.)

See, the thing is, I'm a substance-over-style gal. I've learned to overlook a lot of stuff over the years, as there's often a pearl of wisdom embedded in the debris. Because someone has some flaw or distortion does not mean they don't also have valuable gifts. You've just gotta decide on a case-by-case basis how much weirdness you're willing to pick through.

So, the guy's channeling is not in question for me. His messages are powerful, incisive, insightful, specific, commanding, and astute. They are also not very fun or uplifting. They're a bit dreary and Old Testament for my taste, which is one of the reasons why I stopped going to his group. However, what's with the accents? No, *really*, what's with the accents? Were Shaw and Shakespeare now trying to get in on the action? Why did they take years to make their presence known? Were they waiting for green cards?

At any rate, while at this American/Irish/English channeling convention, I got a flyer for Abdy from the channeler's agent, for Abdy is represented by the same agent. Yes, I know how that sounds. It sounds like that to me, too.

Abdy is an "energy worker," someone who toils in the diffuse realm of that which is invisible to the naked eye, as any physicist does. We may not see the energy itself, but we know it by its fruit, as when wind chimes are animated by a breeze.

My interest in the ethereal spheres challenges me to rely on my own knowing. To come into my own Sovereignty, my Mastery. I invite you to come into yours, too, as Luke did in his "blind" light saber training with Obi Wan Kenobi against a remote in *Return of the Jedi.* This does not mean that we cannot benefit from others' teachings and skills. They can trigger our own understandings, even if they are frauds. We have to be discerning, and not dumb ourselves down in deference to someone else's alleged status or power. If you "feel nothing" in response to a healing or teaching, it may be because there was nothing there to feel. On the other hand, even if you do "feel something," how do you know it's really from them and not from you? And if you don't feel anything, it's still possible that something (either good or bad) still took place. It's a slippery slope when it comes to interpretation. The only one you should really trust at the end of the day is yourself. And that *is* the lesson. That, and to keep an open mind. I'm not advocating distrust of others, but too many people defer to others and give their power away. This is a cardinal sin.

Before Abdy started to work the packed room, he said, "There is no name for what you receive."

I'll say. But there is a name for what he receives. $40. Now, I liked the guy and his "energy," and he certainly didn't hurt me. But he didn't knock me to the ground with his electricity. On the other hand, people around me were swooning and screaming. I felt rather like I was in a madhouse, a classic insane asylum to be exact. Now, to be fair, most of the folk in attendance were well-behaved. But some of the "loosy goosy" types were flapping and flailing, convulsing and twitching Salem witch-trial style. I was feverishly looking around for an exorcist and an exit.

One guy with a beard and big belly broke out in maniacal laughter, rocking and rolling on the floor while the waistband of his sweat pants hovered tenuously around the crack of his butt. Others hooted, cried and wailed. Some even whimpered. An occasional moan or shriek rang out and echoed in the high ceilinged room. Good God. A couple of women sounded like they were having orgasms, and another like she was giving birth, all on a cold church floor. Do I know how to have fun on a Saturday night?

Abdy told us to lie down once we were "touched" by him. But this was too good a show to miss, so I popped right back up to survey what was going on, and to make sure no lunatic snuck up on me and had a rabid seizure, convulsion, or gave birth in my personal space. When one loonie started wailing, another would too, as if in manic competition. A crazed chain reaction would ripple through the room.

Listen, it's easy for me to make fun of them. I don't know what was going on, or what he opened up for them. I don't think it was bad. There are a lot of messed up people who are not in touch with themselves. So, they let Abdy touch them instead.

"If you are sad, the energy will release sad," he said. "If you are mad, the energy will release mad."

I guess I'm wary, cause that's what released. Actually, that's not true. I went in desiring to have a mystical experience, not wanting to rag on lunatics (or to be with them, frankly). I wanted to love Abdy and our "electric exchange," to be bowled over by his energy and to have an ecstatic adventure. While I did feel *something* the second time he touched me (a light tingling in my head when he looked intently in my eyes then touched my third eye with his thumb) overall, I was left cold. I cut out early.

When I asked for feedback regarding the event from my channeler friend Nicole, she focused then declared, "Well, he certainly knows how to move energy. But frankly, there are very few people from whom you can benefit at this time. You're more evolved energetically than most of the people you've been seeking out."

I'm not trying to sound big-headed. I didn't say it. *She* did. On the other hand, I have been studying my whole life. And I am pretty cool. You have to graduate sometime.

I've received messages from Spirit advising me to stop seeking. Sounds crazy, right? Stop seeking *teachers*, they said. I'm not seeking teachers, per se, but strong leaders, interesting people and experiences to ignite my growth and offer unique, new perspectives. Learning never stops. What's wrong with wanting to study with Einstein? Apparently, there's a shortage of good teachers. At least for me. I'm certainly not seeking a guru.

I'm looking for a good time, and I seek it in Spirit, not in bars (although I do enjoy "spirits"). For example, the aforementioned trance medium I studied with. He was sweet, simple, and slow (not mentally, but in manner). Real relaxed like. When it came down to it, I learned more and pushed myself harder when I studied with medium James Van Praagh. A fast-paced New Yorker like myself, he was chock full of exercises and new ideas that kept me on my toes. While his ideas were consistent with what I already knew and felt (this was a plus), he also took me places mentally, spiritually and psychically I *hadn't* yet been. That's why I go to a class, or an event. I want new vistas and challenges and for my world-view to be shaken up.

This applies to tap class (I go regularly) as much as any spoon-bending workshop (I've been to one. Of course). A substitute teacher walked into my tap class and I was immediately perturbed by her dour demeanor. She was "street," slouchy hip-hop grunge. No problem there. However, making no eye contact and looking only at her phone as she entered the room was an "uh oh" for me. Then she plugged her phone into the sound system. Okay, good. At least she would be playing music. Not all tap teachers do.

She smiled finally (thank God) and started leading our warm up, all the while holding a cup of coffee. An intriguing prop, though she did spill once. I wondered if she clutched a cocktail during afternoon classes.

Class dragged as I kept waiting for her to turn on a tune to spice things up. She continued to scroll through tunes on her iPod. Since she made up our routine on the spot, I thought she was probably trying to figure out the perfect piece of music as she improvised.

While lithe, when this gal slammed her taps down the sound reverberated as if from a giant's stride. By comparison, I sounded like a mouse with paperclips taped to my toes. "Not bad," she'd announce to the group. Never a "pretty good" or even "Hey, that was better!" There's such a huge difference between the two approaches and her approach was demoralizing. She never did play music. Turned out she was just charging her phone and checking her damn texts.

Now, on to the meat and potatoes of this piece. My weekend workshop with Panache Desai. Having worked like a dog recording audio books seven days a week up to eighteen hours (on and off) a day for a good eighteen months straight, I finally gave myself a three day break. I bounded off for Port Authority and bonded with others waiting in line for our bus up north, which was late. Finally, the lady standing in front of me in line checked the bus outside and said, "Well, the lights are on and the motor's running."

While our driver was still missing in action, this was nonetheless a very promising sign. I was in great spirits when we arrived at our destination.

I wasn't sure who Panache really was, other than a smiley, young, new age guy. Same as every other personal growth leader with an over bright grin. What was he selling? It was impossible to determine from class literature, which sounded as vague as the "messages" of his smiling, soulful competitors. New age catalogues are full of classes taught by smiling teachers with loving messages. Why should I give any of them my shekels? I can smile in the mirror and love myself without their tutelage. I based my decision to study with him on a very short Internet interview I caught with him and past-life regressionist Dr. Brian Weiss in which Panache seemed appealing, positive and open-minded.

I thought, *Ah, now I know who he is.*

When I found he was offering a class near me, I decided to go. I trusted my intuition and fully expected to like this fellow and to benefit from his workshop.

CHAPTER 4

The Lights are on and the Motor's Running

Part 2
Getting into Gear

Before class even began, I saw Panache Desai in the center's bookshop. I was pleased and almost blurted out to him as he walked by me, "You're my teacher!" But something in me held back. I remained silent and watched him as he strolled past, hypnotically drawn to his own book, CD, and DVD display in the shop. While the room was empty and he was inches away from me, he did not even glance my way. This surprised me for, in my mind, being an open and loving person means being able to make eye contact and comfortably, if not warmly, acknowledge the people around you. At least some of the time. And certainly at a new age joint where you're considered a leader. I reach out with my eyes and energy much of the time in New York City, choosing to expand into the population rather than contract into myself as most people do, hiding behind their sunglasses, eyes trained on their smart phones. But I found this not to be the case with Panache.

Interestingly, I kept bumping into him all weekend,

or perhaps he kept bumping into me. This was a large new age joint I was visiting. Bumping into someone repeatedly was not the norm. He spoke to me in passing in the dining hall about the food. Later, he walked by where I was sitting at the café.

He asked me what time I had and commented with his English accent, "You're a bit ahead."

He was referring to the fact that my watch was five minutes fast, but his observation was also prescient.

Despite being happy to be away from the city and excited for class to start Friday night, I was turned off almost immediately by the very energy he claims (or so I found out) is supposed to heal you just by being in its vicinity. He also affirms that he is enlightened. Oh dear.

While I couldn't argue with about ninety percent of what Panache said, it was stuff that I already knew, having either heard it, read it, thought it, or written it. He did not take me anywhere new. It became clear as he spoke that he's all Panache and no substance, a glib, informal speaker whose words were replete with inconsistencies and contradictions. We did no exercises, nor did we interact with each other, except for some hugging at the very end on Sunday morning. He said we would dance. We never did. He told us we would have fun (that's a big assumption). I did not.

Panache tried to be funny, jocular, and cool (as evidenced by the booming "popular" music he played at length). He set himself up as a healer who would "fix us" and "change our lives forever." A true master would never claim this power over others. He contended that one of his special skills as an enlightened man was his ability to match his (purple) socks with his (purple) sweater. Ha ha. Some people snickered at his attempt at humor. The room was filled with his acolytes. When he continued to drop Oprah's name, this Pudgy Punjabi (I don't know where exactly his family's from beyond homes in India, London, and Florida, but the moniker's got a ring to it) further rubbed me the wrong way.

Did Jesus blow his own horn? If he did, I like to think that he did so in a healthy manner. You can be confident and comfortable at the same time. You can know your worth. Like a math genius simply stating the fact that he is a math genius, as Alan Turing does in *The Imitation Game*.

Panache asserted that everything about us is divine and perfect, including our moods (no matter how miserable), our pain, foibles, and inconsistencies (he should know about that one). "If you're feeling rage or despair, just sit with it," he advised. "Stop thinking and simply be in the heart." He assured us that doing this was all very simple, without explaining the nature of the simplicity.

I agree that every bit of us is divine, but not with his directive to simply sit with your pain and neither express nor analyze it.

Personal problems are not simply released. You have to determine what is wrong, and why. When you don't deal with toxic emotions they fester and grow like gangrene. In order to heal, something has to shift into a new gear. Something has to move. He provided us with no tools with which to help ourselves, but presented himself as the tool that would uplift us, just by being in proximity to him. He was the drug his followers would continue to need, and a drug pusher no better than Big Pharma.

Pain is a signal that something is wrong, either in what is happening, or in our reaction to it. If I'm furious, I alleviate my distress either by changing the situation I'm pissed about or adjusting my response to it. If I'm sad, I work to mitigate that mood. I seek relief. There are reasons for everything we feel and do. Our feelings are the result of our beliefs about an event. We have the ability to analyze our thoughts, beliefs and behaviors and to make changes in our lives so that we feel better. We can stop stepping in land mines and we can also avoid creating them. You don't stand in quicksand and simply wait to be sucked down. You do something.

While people don't necessarily need years of therapy for everything, a certain amount of processing is required to move through stuff. You can use tools like books, friends, therapists, and you can meditate and journal. Once you start to trust yourself, you will master and utilize your own inner resources to figure out what is going on by asking yourself questions. After strides have been made in the loving and accepting of yourself, sure, then you can make quicker, easier switches out of despair into relief, a swift right turn down the road to release instead of a hard left toward resentment.

But when we first learn a skill it requires effort, and that can frustrate us impatient modern-day types. Toddlers don't get upset when learning to walk because they don't have judgments about not doing it perfectly, nor do they have fears of failure. They just pick themselves up and try again, moving towards what they want. We adults, however, trip ourselves up. We can learn how to get out of our own way over time by consciously changing our behavior, including mental habits. You don't just get in a racing car and take a pro spin your very first try.

And while we in the West may think too much and get stuck in our heads, God didn't give us a brain and logic for nothing. The head and the heart are designed to work in concert, just as the body and the spirit are. They are a powerful team when allowed to work in tandem.

Panache's suggestion that we "let it be" is akin to acknowledging that poop is a normal, healthy bodily function. While this is true, you don't have to sit in it.

You could perhaps blame some of my irritability in class on the fact that I did not sleep terribly well in my bunk bed near the bathroom (convenient for a nocturnal pee-er like myself, but noisy) and right by the (glaringly bright) red EXIT sign, and also due to the fact that someone in our large dorm room saw fit to rearrange her entire velcro, tin foil, and zipper collection at five a.m. Breakfast was not for another two hours, and I was now decidedly awake, agitated, and starving. I hate being hungry. I might as well have scheduled surgery and put the starvation to good use.

Something had also awakened me after midnight, and after I rearranged my bedding and my thoughts, I took in my surroundings. I twisted around to stare out the cold window at a sight I'm not privy to in Manhattan, a November sky brimming with stars. While much of my gratitude and joy at being away was now out the window, a little bit seeped back in with this starry vista.

At dawn, of all things, I wet my bed. No, I didn't pee. As I dressed, the contents of my water bottle seeped out onto the mattress. I'd been so assiduous about not committing noise crimes like Velcro the Ripper and other noise philistines in the room that I refrained from creating excess noise by not screwing my water bottle completely shut.

Fortunately, the room was sauna-like enough to dehydrate my mattress by nightfall.

I raced to the dining hall and nibbled ravenously (is this possible?) on a "healthy" pumpkin muffin with a mystery ingredient I finally concluded was sand. However, all this was not the true source of my ultimate crankiness. My "class" was.

"Panache has an ability to help people to move through their sadness, anger, or fear to once again come back to their infinite potential. No matter your life experience, your spiritual background, or role, Panache can help you." (from his website)

Contrary to his claim of being able to offer relief, I saw many people bottled up with frustration as they tried to express their concerns only to have him shut them down mid-sentence so that he could continue to talk.

Also to my shock and dismay, Panache casually admitted to being full of shit and then accused us all of being the same. I don't appreciate being insulted by teachers, be they tap dancers or happiness coaches. Had the course description divulged that he was an "enlightened guru who was full of shit," I could have saved some money. Panache complained that being enlightened was both boring and bland.

Then he jokingly challenged us to join him, "If I have to do it, then you do, too!"

Where do I sign up? Was Jesus bored? The Buddha? They never mentioned it.

After the screening I attended of *The Imitation Game* there was a Q&A with the cast. They were asked "How do you deal with poorly written roles?"

Sophisticated Charles Dance apologetically offered, "There's *just* so much you can do."

Also, with a delightful English accent (the lot of them had, the movie takes place in England), handsome Matthew Goode piped up, "You can't polish a turd."

Okay, not so sophisticated a response. However, ever the brilliant wordsmiths, the Irish, Allen Leech (of *Downton Abbey* fame, the chauffeur turned widower) chimed in with his brogue, "No, but you can roll it in glitter."

Touché.

When I encounter such substances, I don't polish or dress them up. I don't wade, wallow in or play with them. I flush.

I sat by myself at lunch, but sought out two nearby

classmates and joined them. "Are you enjoying yourselves in class?"

They both nodded, then one came back with, "Are you?"

Pause. "I'm not."

The older gal seemed miffed. "Well, you're not supposed to enjoy yourself!" she returned.

The younger one was pretty, blonde, and Russian. She remained mostly mute during the following exchange.

"I'm not?" I replied, genuinely shocked.

"No, you're not. It's not about that."

"Oh? What is it about?"

"He's changing us on an energetic level."

He is? What's he doing? I didn't sign up for any psychic surgery or mystery modifications. "How does he do that?" I queried.

She practically rolled her eyes at me. "Just by *being* with him!"

Oh, right. He's that special. Doesn't even have to touch you. Doesn't even bother to *look* at his followers, like Braco does, or touch them like Abdy. We have to look at *him*. I'm paying the money and I have to do all the damn work.

"Well, I came here to have a good time," I persisted. "I like to enjoy my classes, and I certainly like to like my teachers."

She pounced on me again. "He's not even a teacher!"

This lady was contrary, plain and simple. Clearly he hadn't cleared *her* cranky-ass energy field, and she'd been to his seminars numerous times. There's no guru powerful enough to clean up a sour personality that refuses to work on itself. Inspiring people is one thing. Overhauls are for car mechanics.

"He just *vibrates*!" As if that explained everything.

"So do you," I replied.

She was even angrier now, her vibrations approaching the ferocity of a space shuttle preparing for launch. My insides were gripping. So much for a healthy lunch. There's not enough kale in the world to compensate for a World Wrestling Federation match in your stomach.

"You don't understand. He just *is*. He fixes us with his vibration," she patronized.

To which I replied, "Well, I didn't come here to be fixed. I came here to have a good time, and I'll appreciate your not telling me how I should experience my weekend or my class."

She breathed out with heavy exasperation, "Ugh! This is *not* supposed to be fun! You *just* don't get it!" she deposited into the thick air then got up to leave, her Siberian sycophant in tow. I was not amongst peers.

People in class yearned for relief. You could hear it in their quavering voices, in their questions and stories, but he cut them off after a sentence or two with a facile response. One lady complained about being hit up for money by a friend.

"Just say no," he blurted.

While indeed that is a terrific response, the fact that, by her own admission, it was a recurring issue in her life, that she felt used, unappreciated for who she was but was wanted only what she could offer financially, "just say no" was a glib suggestion. Self-esteem and learning to stand up for herself would seem to be the deeper issues.

When someone asked about karma, he dropped, "Karma is a mind fuck" without explaining the meaning or nature of his bomb.

He advised folks to "just let it go," "sit with the rage," "it's all because your father didn't pay attention to you," (which the speaker never even mentioned).

You could see the frustration in people's faces when

he interrupted them while they were sharing. They needed, at the very least, to be heard, if not understood or helped. It takes courage for most people to stand up in a large group of strangers and share personal problems, but their bravery went unrewarded. He even encouraged one woman who was afraid of sinking into a depressive state again to consciously seek the state of depression out. This is not professional advice. Facing your problems is different from running toward them. Heroin is not the solution when you're an addict trying to get clean. He invited questions, but as soon as someone started sharing a sensitive issue he silenced them with a facile response or, "Come here. I'm going to hug you." As if his hug was a cure-all.

His groupies went up, doe-eyed, for their blessing. The class catered to his ego, not to the participants who sought relief from this perfunctory "master." I sat in the front row every day, arms crossed, and refused even to look at him.

I said nothing. I wasn't there to teach him, or challenge him. It was his "class." Or "energy event." Or whatever the hell it was.

He also came up with the brilliant, "The more love you feel, the more fear you'll feel."

How does that work? And why would anyone want to become more loving if they're going to become more fearful? This is contradictory to every spiritual tenet not to mention my own personal experience. The more love you feel, the LESS fear you feel. They cannot exist in the same space. When you're brimming with love, you're practically fearless.

He ended class with a big hug-in. First by offering his own hug to individuals, as a healing modality, of course. Like a big plastic pacifier.

"I'm having feelings of deep unresolved guilt involving my father, who recently passed away. I want to—" someone started to confess before he cut her off with, "Come here. I'm going to give you a hug."

Wow, one hug and everything gets washed away? I was edging toward the back of the room by now, determined to escape early and participate in a group Skype session with my friend Nicole, the channeler. He had already hugged about five people at the front of the room, when he encouraged mass huggings among the participants.

I noticed a man in the back with glasses on. He had an urban, artistic air to him, and didn't quite look as if he belonged in this granola-ish group. When a woman approached to hug him, he swiftly backed away.

"I'm not a hugger," he bristled, then abruptly walked out. I smiled and left minutes later, an hour before class officially ended.

When I finally got Nicole's two cents on the situation, via her guides, I was yet again bowled over by the unexpected nature of Spirit's observations. Nicole said, "You're gonna laugh your pants off and want money from this man, but you're there to help *him*, that's the reason you're there. You're helping him energetically. He's not going to acknowledge you or compensate you for it, but you have something he needed to get to his next level. He called to you energetically, and you answered the call. You worked with him in another lifetime. He rubbed you the wrong way now just like he frustrated you in the past. But he needs your consciousness for his growth. This is a teacher-student relationship and you're the teacher. There is a greater purpose beyond what you can see, a real reason you're there this weekend. Your consciousness is going to help him to grow. On a higher level, he thanks you, for he needed your help."

Son of a gun. I guess that "being in the presence of

someone's energy" stuff that he claims to do really works, cause that's apparently what I did for him for three days. He's the one raking in all the money. He needs *my* help, which he gets, then I pay him to boot! Good one.

Nicole's guides continued, "You're looking for something to delight you, but it's not in these classes. It's time for you to do the inner work and stop seeking answers outside."

Shit. They told me to meditate and write, and that I need to energetically *feel* my way through life, and vibrate higher.

They challenged me, "If you are the Master, then what do you know? You need to be hell bent on developing your own class, curriculum, books and channelings, and stop seeking out others. Be like Madonna, and follow the beat of your own drum. Madonna listens to Madonna and nobody else. It's time for you to do that, too. You have her potential if you want it, but you can't achieve it if you think others know more than you do. You're an amazing coach. It's time to coach yourself."

I was not there to seek acclaim or tenure. I was simply someone who wanted to have a pleasant weekend and ended up as the gal grumbling in the back.

This was a rather heavy charge they were saddling me with. *You mean I can't just sit in class anymore? I gotta take the stage?* Yup. While daunting, their message hit home. I'm smart, funny, comfortable speaking, teaching, entertaining, and I've been a "student" of enlightenment, happiness, and personal growth my whole life. It's time for me to step up to the plate. Gulp.

They continued, "Start working with your Guides one on one. Stop looking outside of yourself. Masters consult with other Masters. Work within. There's no need to go to Tibet. You are determined to believe that 'they' all have something you want. Just because someone has a following or fancy ad does not mean that they know more than you, or can help you. If you like what they do, then start your own course, your own spiritual class, your own channeling. Write your next book, your next play, audition people to be on staff for *your* next project. Go within! Your former students are coming to you for instruction. What does this tell you? Where are you? Who are you? You are, in fact, The Master. Start to believe it, and gain more confidence in this area. Meditate. Write what you receive. You will channel your own prose. Not with your logical mind, but you will feel your way to the higher energies."

Shut off the logical mind? Try telling that to a fast-paced smarty pants New Yorker.

They concluded, "Stop being a spiritual groupie. They are few and far between that have something to teach you. Meditate. Meditate. Meditate. Listen to your own Inner Voice."

This unsettled me. I have to go back to school. Rather, I have to start one.

As a final insult, on my last day away I got a huge piece of the driest, cheapest, stringiest dental floss stuck in my teeth. And who provided me with this flimsiest of floss? My freaking dentist. Someone offered me a toothpick and advised me never to use waxed floss, only unwaxed.

"It *was* unwaxed, that's *why* it got stuck."

That and the fact that it was thinner than optical fiber. Though ephemeral enough to disintegrate while on the job, when lodged in my mouth for hours, it felt like a mile of nautical rope.

Before I left I said goodbye to my bunkmate and asked her to pray for me.

"For your mate to appear?"

"No, for the floss to dislodge." It took pliers and a piece of waxed floss to get the offending fiber out of my mouth when I got home.

Despite my disappointment with the "class," I rallied my mood while away. It was, after all, my weekend. So I put my "tools" to use, adjusted my attitude and had a good time anyway.

My quest for inspiration and fun landed me squarely back at my own door, just like Dorothy with her ruby slippers.

Dorothy: "Oh, will you help me? Can you help me?"
Glinda: "You don't need to be helped any longer. You've always had the power to go back to Kansas."
Dorothy: "I have?"
Scarecrow: "Then why didn't you tell her before?"
Glinda: "She wouldn't have believed me. She had to learn it for herself."
Scarecrow: "What have you learned, Dorothy?"
Dorothy: "Well, I—I think that it, that it wasn't enough just to want to see Uncle Henry and Auntie Em—and it's that—if I ever go looking for my heart's desire again, I won't look any further than my own backyard. Because if it isn't there, I never really lost it to begin with! Is that right?"
Glinda: "That's all it is!"
Scarecrow: "But that's so easy! I should've thought of it for you—"
Tin Man: "I should have felt it in my heart—"
Glinda: "No, she had to find it out for herself. Now those magic slippers will take you home in two seconds!"
Dorothy: "Oh! Toto, too?"
Glinda: "Toto, too."
Dorothy: "Now?"
Glinda: "Whenever you wish."

Dorothy: "Now."

Glinda: "Then close your eyes and tap your heels together three times. And think to yourself, 'There's no place like home.'"

I don't need to be hugged, stared at, or energetically knocked down by someone else. Neither do you.

My motor's running.

My lights are on.

CHAPTER 5

Burn

I'm going to tackle everybody's favorite topic today, death and dying! What could be more fun than that? The fact is, I consider myself rather a death expert. As painful as it is to lose loved ones (I've got a PhD in the field), I have never shied away from the understanding that death is inevitable, not something to be fought at all costs (obviously, this is decided by individuals on a case-by-case basis).

For, in fact, we all get to die someday! And believe me, you will find it to be a relief and great pleasure when you get to the other side, like taking off a tight pair of shoes at the end of a long day. Our consciousness goes on forever for energy can neither be created nor destroyed. Your sense of self existed before you were born and will continue after you release your mortal coil. It's only the body that dies, but this is good news. Who wants to be you forever? Can you imagine your life story (and body) going on indefinitely? Change is good. When you "die" you get to expand your awareness of who you are, and stop playing the same role and wearing the same costume daily. It gets old.

The body morphs continuously. From the day you're born the clock starts ticking. We consider the first forty years or so of aging to be acceptable and cute (you're coming into your own, growing to maturity, developing your power) and the last forty (or sixty) years of change to be "not so cute," despite the accretion of wisdom and experience. We are no different from flowers that bloom then wither. What's so bad about that? Consider that, while no one likes the idea of dying, death itself may really not be so bad. It's a release, pure and total freedom from limitation, care, and pain, like jumping off a Hawaiian cliff into pure, refreshing water. Energizing, liberating, and beautiful.

I recently referred to one of my gym teachers as middle-aged. "You know, she's fifty or sixty."

My friend's husband said, "Sixty is not middle-aged."

"Well, people die at seventy, right? So, middle aged is what, thirty-five?"

You wanna be called middle-aged at thirty and a senior at sixty, go ahead. Not me, sucker! I'm just me. The numbers change. I don't. Though I do get cuter, wiser, more playful and fun. Time is a vehicle that allows us to morph, and time has served me well. Are you allowing it to serve you? That's what it's here for. Time and space are psychological constructs, and the aging body is a reminder that we are not here forever. A body comes with built in planned obsolescence. Human existence is a limited time offer. So make hay (or wine) while the sun shines. Put your time to good use. It's not just about shopping, showing off your fabulous life on social media and getting plastic surgery, for God's sake. That's obsessing about the ephemeral you, your persona in this one lifetime, and not about the Real You playing the part.

By me, middle-age is a vague, useless, and insulting

term. It's neither here nor there, neither up nor down. There are only two kinds of ages as far as I'm concerned. You're younger or older, alive or dead, how's that? And from what I hear, you're more alive in many ways when you're dead than when you're in a physical body. Dying is relief, like sinking into a hot bath. Think of how heavy you feel after you come out of water. You're leaden. That's physical life. Leaving your body makes you leaven, so you can go to heaven (sue me). And how many people do you know that walk around like the living dead anyway? There's a reason zombie movies are so popular these days.

Read *The Afterlife of Billy Fingers* by Annie Kagan for an uplifting, surreal, and psychedelic perspective of the afterlife. And for those who are intrigued with this field, try *Saved by the Light* by Dannion Brinkley. Having physically died and come back (in a hospital, where it was medically verified), he's now an Advocate of the After World in hospices. He works as a cheerleader of sorts, a Lobbyist for Life Everlasting, reassuring those that are close to transitioning that a wild and wonderful ride awaits them. And for more incredible insight and inspiration into both life and death, read Anita Moorjani's *Dying to be Me*. There's more to all of us than meets the eye.

The constantly transforming body is an invitation to remember that you are not the physical form. You are having an experience *of* life *through* the body, like a tourist on a cruise ship, from which you disembark when you're done with the ride. It's that simple. Just bounce off the boat. You're still you. You never were the vessel, but it allowed you to have unique experiences by offering new vistas through its portholes. The body cycles through seasons just like everything else on this planet. Spring, summer, fall and winter. But out of death and winter life springs again. That's how we roll here on Planet Earth.

Jesus is the God of Resurrection, and so are we. Easter is a sweet celebration of the fact that death is an illusion and life always renews.

We die a little every day. We leave bits of our bodies behind when we go to the bathroom, releasing undigested food, toxins, and dead cells so we can renew, rebuild, and refresh in the now. We release used breath and take in the new. When your hair is cut, you leave it behind and walk away from what is no longer wanted. The hair on the floor is not you. You don't hold burial services for it. You are consciousness. Try and maintain a lighter (but loving) relationship with your form.

The subtle bodily changes that happen daily are a continuous process we pay no attention to. They are little deaths. Little births. We are constantly regenerating, revitalizing and rebooting. Yet a part of you remains changeless. It is not your body. It's using the body to see, feel, hear, and experience physical life. Your body is a "virtual reality" device.

We don't make monuments to our offal. So why do we do so with our ultimate "bm" the "body movement" of releasing spirit from matter, and allow the body to go to the recycling plant like we do with old cars? Why don't we "flush"? Because we over identify with the body, the ego and personality, but these are merely aspects of our physical life, not our True Self. People get attached to their cars and homes too, but if you want the new (or even if you don't) you have to release the old eventually or you'll end up a hoarder. Change is inevitable. Growth is optional. Allow yourself to be up-cycled, both physically and psychologically.

I watched the one-hour documentary *A Will For The Woods* about the green burial movement. The film made me a bit nauseous (I'm not big on corpses) and maudlin. My mother died of cancer when I was twenty-two, and I was intimately involved in her day-to-day care until the end, working with a hospice. I also shopped around for her cremation while she was dying, a bitterly hard task if ever there was one. When I shared my movie recommendation with friends, it struck a real chord with many. There's something grievously wrong with our current funeral practices, both financially, and environmentally.

This is an important issue for people to ponder. The embalming process and our over-the-top funeral industry is incredibly toxic to the environment. The concept of "preserving the remains" is something folks really have to think about, too. The soul has left. The body disintegrates and becomes new life, if we let it do so naturally. "Preserves" are for fruit, not people. *A Will for the Woods* shows how we can *nourish* the land with green burial practices, instead of littering it with chemicalized corpses and casket parking lots. When someone starts a green burial ground in the film, a forest is saved from being clear-cut.

A Family Undertaking is also a fine documentary about families performing natural home rituals for their dead the way many do with home births. There are even certified death "midwives."

Funerals, like weddings, are big business. And they are not unrelated. There's often something to prove in both cases, keeping up with the Joneses, trying to impress, trying to prove how much you loved your dead (maybe you did, maybe you didn't, but you can certainly put on a good show). And show it is. My uncle was laid out to rest holding a rosary, and while he could hardly be called a regular churchgoer, don't you think the funeral home could have at least gotten the religion of the dead guy right? He was Greek Orthodox, not Catholic (though my cousin said the rosary was appropriate, I don't understand why. Greeks play with worry beads, not rosaries.)

No disrespect to my uncle (I adored him) but leaving a TV remote control in that casket would have been more representative than a rosary. We need to invest in life, not death, and in *marriage*, not weddings. (I like a nice party, but you know what I mean).

I'm particularly perplexed by the way Christians cling to the corpse. Seems hypocritical, since they believe the soul is eternal. So why do they hold on to the cast off shell? Worshipping the corpse is illogical. It's false idolatry. And, yes, I get it, more than logic is involved here, but the "dead look" alone should clue mourners in to the fact that the person they loved is no longer there. The house they knew is barely standing, it's propped up with stilts, and no one is home. Anyone who's ever seen the corpse of their loved one knows the vacated body is a poor facsimile of the live version. No better than a simulated figure in a wax museum (and usually, a lot worse).

The time to throw money at the dead is when they're ALIVE. You think their spirit is really gonna' care about all the cash you throw at their cold dead body? How about indulging and embracing your loved ones roundly while they're still ambulatory? How about investing in your *own* life? Where are *you* holding back?

The time to respect the body is when it is alive. The body is merely a means of transportation. Is your car squeaky clean or a hot mess? A car says a lot about its owner, and so does a body. Do you feed yours well? Give it exercise? Do you nourish it emotionally, love it, give it rest, care, offer it peace and well-being, or do you run it off the road in a vain attempt to achieve "perfection" or to escape life altogether? I'm talking about those who can't sit still, who can't "be" in their bodies, who must "do, do, do" all the time. They are trying to get out of their bodies, running endlessly, exercising forever, punishing, pushing, denying and depriving. If you did this to an animal (and many do) it would be called abuse. We all need rest and recreation, peace, joy and *fun*. There is tremendous discomfort in this world, and much of it originates with our uneasiness with the human vehicle itself, our home while we're physically alive. All the plastic surgery in the world won't keep you from dying. Think of your body as your pet or your child. Treat it with kindness, compassion and care.

We worship or abhor the flesh. The Church declared the world dirty and sinful (and women in particular since we generate life here, which, in fact, makes us God), and we've been punishing our physical selves ever since. Since it's been already condemned, we relegate it to its sinful purposes, sex, degeneracy, and death. Hence our obsession with pornography, fetishes, pedophilia, bestiality, violence, terror, blood, cruelty, and more blood. If we're in a sinful world, we might as well dance with the devil, right? What the hell is going on? Fear and contempt of the physical realm (including our environment) is what's going on, and the Church is responsible in great part for this disgraceful attitude, including the belief in the Apocalypse (many of them can't wait for it to happen, and are doing all they can to bring it about with endless war and utter contempt for Mother Nature). The ecclesiastical premise for this attitude is absurd, for God created this world, and if it's bad then blame the manufacturer. Those who understand that Spirit IS Everything understand the world's Divine, if ephemeral, nature. The world is illusory. Transitory. Magical. Mysterious. Magnificent. And here for a purpose.

Though the Church may have started this ugly trend of bodily and worldly hatred, we've sustained this bias by not questioning it. As a result, we have poisoned the physical world by showing it no respect whatsoever. The physical is merely a lower (denser, heavier, not *bad*) vibrational representation of the higher, heavenly realms. Think of it as a Xerox copy of an original masterpiece. But we *can* create Heaven on Earth, and I believe that is our charge as stewards of this planet. Clearly God does not control this realm. We do. We are God's children, God's proxies, God's representatives here. Let's live up to our noble legacy instead of trashing the playpen. When we treat the world like a masterpiece, it responds as one.

People don't like decay. We want everything squeaky clean, germ free and brand spanking new in our culture, including dead corpses and live women who are pressured to douche, diet, pluck, weave, braid, extend, sanitize, bleach, reduce, enhance, remove, wax, deodorize, dye and paint their natural born selves. Most of these chemical cosmetic processes, we are now learning, are carcinogenic. What are the ultimate ramifications of injecting our bodies with Restalyne and Botox? It's embalming the body while it's alive.

While I'm opposed to worshipping the flesh, am I against honoring its beauty via athletics, dance, yoga and a good haircut? Of course not. It's all a matter of balance. It's also a matter of intentionality. Are you running *toward* something? (health, feeling good, experience, adventure, creation) or are you running *away* from something (I don't want to be fat, old, ugly, invisible, yada yada). Therein lies the difference. It's intentionality and moderation that count. You can't run full marathons three days in a row. You must know how to modulate your efforts—when to push your car into fifth gear; when to coast, cruise; get maintenance; or park it in the garage.

As a testament to what the human soul can do with an "imperfect" body, watch this incredible short story of a remarkable young man (look up Steep Your Soul, Meet Chris, Super Soul Sunday, Oprah Winfrey Network on Youtuble).

And look up this piece about a remarkable older one, Paul Smith, typewriter artist, Oregon nursing home, Youtube.

When I was growing up I was shocked to learn that the "women" I admired on the cover of Vogue and other magazines were not, in fact, women at all. They were girls. Children. Brooke Shields was a perfect example of this pedophilic idolatry. To dress our daughters up like sexually active women is unfair to them (let them be children!) and to women (already considered too old at twenty-five when the gold standard is twelve), we are always striving to be what we are not, never content with what and who we are. But that is what we do. We worship at the altar of youth, a brief chimera. It's why pedophilia is rampant and companies like American Apparel have such appalling ad campaigns. We reject the full, soft, mature female body. We want skinny, pubescent, and firm. Women's bodies are watery, and, as such, they ripple and flow. We are ruled by the moon and connected to the stars.

This burden applies increasingly now to young men who must feel grossly inadequate if they don't look like Hollister or Abercrombie models. This is what the American Dream has devolved into, not to be educated, free, happy, creative, curious, unencumbered, inventive, productive, and bold human beings, but to have abs, asses and boobs. We've become plastic Ken and Barbie Dolls, plastic surgeried GI Joes and Josephines. We have allowed ourselves to be dumbed down by Madison Ave. And who rules it? The Media. And who rules that? The Corporations who run our Corporatocracy. Who *are* the men behind the curtain? We may never find out, but we have to connect the dots, use our noggins, and fight the power.

It is time to wake up and claim our rightful legacy as

children of God. Every one of us.

We have been strategically led away from our true power as human beings, and reduced to our body parts, no better than inventory at an auto body shop. Silicone lips, boob jobs, liposuction, butt implants. Is this how you want to be remembered when you die? Vain attempts to keep the car looking brand new, even though it's got 100,000 miles on it, instead of appreciating where the car has been? I love Georgia O' Keefe, in part because she painted bones and artistically embraced her womanly self as she aged. If you haven't seen the flick *Death Becomes Her* (a very black comedy with Goldie Hawn and Meryl Streep) do yourself a favor and rent it.

I watched a documentary about belly-dancing. As with most women and girls, I've struggled life long with body image. To watch these gals celebrate their curves and love handles was a wonder to me. One of the best troupes in this video was called "Fat Chance Belly Dance." Some of the women were smaller, but two at least were larger, what we might term "fat" in our culture. They were terrific dancers and animated their bodies, jiggle and all, with gusto. I was in awe of their joyous abandon.

"This is the wrong century to be a woman. The best time to have been a woman was when Rubens was a painter, The Fat Century. In that period, if you weighed three hundred pounds you could be a *model*. Christie Brinkley would've been a hatcheck girl. Roseanne - Miss Milan, 1537. In that century you could really have an attitude: 'What d'ya mean, no dessert? I've got a sitting with Caravaggio. If that man doesn't see some cellulite, I'm history. Now hand me that cannoli!" Joy Behar.

Back to the burial show. Frankly, the thought of rotting in the ground gives me the heebie-jeebies. Even though I know that my body won't be me when I've left it, it will still sort of look like I did, but in a really, *really* bad way. It's your Zombie clone, unless you've been embalmed and gussied up by some stylist for the dead, aka, the undertaker. I cannot comprehend that creepy business at all, or doctors who perform autopsies. Frankly, I can't fathom fishing around in the body medically while someone's alive. Yes, I am somewhat squeamish. I have my own discomforts with the body. Brilliantly engineered and executed? Yes. Squishy and weird? Also, yes.

Who are we kidding with the post-mortem makeup? That corpse ain't blushing and you and I both know it. The rosy glow is anything but natural or "healthy" (how can you be both healthy and dead?).

I'm all for disposing of the deceased in a nice timely fashion when they're gone. I was raised a Theosophist with the understanding that it takes a full twenty-four hours for all the various energy systems of the soul and consciousness to depart the body, so it's best not to disturb it before then (this would include embalming and cremation). So, let your corpse rest for a day, take a little nap if you will (death may be a breeze, but dying can be exhausting!) then take care of business. Out with the trash. Better yet, compost. A green burial allows the natural cycles of life and death to create new life out of the old. People are getting inventive with their burial ideas. Although simply planting a tree on top of a corpse would work just as well as this contrived idea (look up "Organic Burial Pods Will Turn Your Loved Ones Into Trees" on the Internet.)

And there's a cute gal, Jae Rhim Jee, who's designed a mushroom-covered eco-suit for corpses that will remove toxins from the body as it merges with the earth. It's an interesting take on zombie fashion design. Look up *Huffington Post* "Mushroom Death Suits" on the Internet.

I do have my limits, however, with the green thing. The folk in these natural burial films want to hang out with their dead for a couple of days, and they're on their own there. I did it once or twice with a cat, I sat (okay, slept) comfortably with their bodies in my home for one night, but that's because they looked nice and peaceful, like they were sleeping. In the morning blood had started oozing out of one cat's nose (where, from her brain?!) and I was like, "That's it! You're in the bag!" I laid her to rest in the woods, as I did with my dog and other cat. They become part of the natural process of decay and reabsorption into new life forms. Cat composting.

The corpses in the home burial films looked lousy, frankly. Yellow, bloated, and well, um, dead. You think I want people seeing me like that? I barely want folk to see me while I'm alive. Bloated, cold, jaundiced, and well, *dead*, is not how I wish to be remembered. No, sirree. Fire me up.

Now *A Will For the Woods* asserts that cremation in the US is also environmentally unsound, as it involves heavy fuel usage to produce high heat over long periods of time. Well, can't we improve on that? What do they do in India? They roll their dead in chickpea flour, wrap them in cheesecloth, pour on sesame oil and toss a lit clove cigarette on the pile (yes, I'm joking, but their process is basic). With just a little kindling, lighter fluid, and a "Duraflame For The Dead," the perfect bonfire can be yours. That's the ultimate "release party," isn't it?

Costco may even come up with a cremation starter kit. Hell, they already sell caskets by the checkout area. "Do you want fries with that casket?" Talk about one-stop shopping. From diapers to deathbeds.

Green people get very granola with this stuff, as with natural childbirth (I certainly wouldn't be a placenta eater) and that's their prerogative. But I am not hanging out with a corpse, embalmed or not. I like the idea of a nice blaze. Fire is purifying. Surely we can legitimize a greener way of burning our dead. Didn't Salem, Massachusetts specialize in this for a while? The American South also perfected its own racist version of the "roast."

The closest I've come to a home cremation was the time I roasted marshmallow Peeps over my stovetop burner because they're so utterly flavorless otherwise. It felt a bit lurid blackening the sugary bodies of tiny yellow chicks and pink bunnies. But they did taste better.

All that being said, I rather love cemeteries, particularly old ones. There is a great peace there, a sense that the "game" is over, but that life itself is not. No more rushing around, worrying or competing. As Lily Tomlin said in her brilliant book and Broadway show (both written with Jane Wagner), *The Search for Intelligent Life in the Universe*, "The thing about the rat race is that even if you win, you're still a rat."

Slash and burn is an agricultural method to clear forest for farming. Mother Nature uses this technique too. From death comes life. From fire, fertility. Obliteration of the old makes way for the new. Don't be clingy and constipated. Be willing to release who you are to embrace who you could be, both literally and metaphorically. Set yourself free, and fly.

CHAPTER 6

The Puppy Song

I attended an all day workshop with Dr. Brian Weiss, an eminent Yale psychiatrist who was totally skeptical of anything "otherworldly" until a patient went back farther in time than he intended her to during a hypnotic regression. She shot straight out of this lifetime and landed smack dab into another. She also started accessing her consciousness between lifetimes, when her wise Oversoul was not identified with any ego, body or persona. This Oversoul provided specific, personal information to Dr. Weiss that no one in the world besides he and his wife knew. Given increasing quantities of verifiable evidence offered during sessions with this gal, his worldview began to shift until he is now the Daddy-O of past-life regression. Two thousand people attended his event in New York City with me. His books, including *Many Lives, Many Masters*, are international bestsellers. The reincarnation movement, which was already huge worldwide, is growing.

My last chapter was about death; game over, phooey, you're kaput. This chapter is about what happens after crossing over, the continuity of life via changing form:

birth, death, regeneration, renewal and rebirth. A case in point. After losing all three of my pets over the last few years, I recently replenished my full supply. Ya'll know about my two new kittens. When I picked my kittens the shelter gave me a used pet knapsack to take them home in (talk about embarrassing, at least for me it was. Wearing it was right up there with pushing a doggie stroller). When I got home, I discovered the knapsack, undoubtedly donated to the shelter by someone whose dog died, had two rawhide dog treats tucked inside a pocket. I was startled by this. It felt like a powerful sign from Spirit, and initiated a new line of thinking, I got cats again (against my better judgment) and I could just as well do the same (against my better judgment) with another dog. It felt foolhardy and wrong, but no one was stopping me (except me). This was a liberating if scary thought. But the prospect of more life, more bills, more responsibility, and yes, eventually, more death, made my stomach churn. Also, how could I replace the perfect dog? Mimi had been like a soulmate. Our compatibility and simpatico had been heaven sent.

Before my acquisition of a new clan I was pet-free for the first time in decades. I was miserable. Bereft. Beside myself. Depressed. I didn't leave my house for days at a stretch. But I didn't want new pets. I missed the ones I'd lost. Angela (cat), Mimi (dog), and Wilbur (cat) were irreplaceable. I'd already made the decision that I should spring for a husband next time, not a dog, that it was time for a human tribe, not an animal one. I worked without cease at home, recording audio books. Like someone on an endless march, I'd become the walking dead.

Eight months of extreme, excruciating grief netted nothing but an incredible body of work recording audio books and a thyroid condition. Stress and grief are not great for the health.

The "dog/husband" debate continued. Knowing full well I was tiptoeing into a danger zone, I joined an online dachshund adoption list. I cringed when the emails came in. I knew I shouldn't even look. It was Puppy Porn. And I was relieved when they were ugly or unappealing. Phew. Saved by the bell.

I'd gone through the same doubting rigamarole before and after adopting the kittens. But after working through my fears, tears, and the kittens' initial health issues (there were those bills I'd worried about!) the three of us settled down, and I started to fall in love with them. It didn't happen immediately, and it usually doesn't, no matter how cute a guy, girl, or kitten is. You have to get to know someone to love them truly. Time affords that opportunity.

But every so often one of the dachshund pups would be so gosh darn cute I'd become obsessed. My heart would flutter. Their adorableness evoked Mimi's adorableness. When they looked like that, I didn't have a choice, which is what happened with Cedric. I filled out the application, knowing I was insane, but damn the torpedoes. I wrote an email to the shelter and followed up with another message through the adoption site. No response. I was crushed. And relieved. No, I was crushed, and anxious, and I still wanted Cedric. Silence ensued.

More ugly pup photos poured in. Really, no different from Internet dating. "Is he cute? Could he be 'the one'?"

Nope. More deletions. Then I became obsessed with another cutie pie, Peanut. He had three hairs sticking up on the top of his head and reminded me of a Charlie Brown Christmas tree. I reached out again to the same shelter, half-heartedly now, despite his cuteness. "I'm interested." Why get my hopes up when they didn't even bother to respond the first time? At least inform me that the dog's no longer available. More resounding silence.

Rude, but I couldn't afford to alienate the agency by telling them what I thought of their lack of professionalism. They still seemed to hold the rusty key to my facacta puppy pipe dream.

My fears escalated along with my hopes. "What are you doing? Don't do it! Don't mess with things! Your life is good! Don't ruin it! You got cats, it's enough. What's next, the hippopotamus?"

There were no mature adults around to talk sense into me. As if sense has anything to do with things like falling in love or getting a puppy.

Another heartbreaker invaded my inbox. Zane. My friends cooed adoringly.

"He looks like a muppet!" opined one pal.

Of course I had to get him, right? He was too cute not to. I filled out another application. An old lady friend of mine who was crazy about Mimi, took one look at his photo and said, "Oh, Valerie, he's adorable. You have to call the shelter."

I didn't want to interfere *too* much since I was still totally on the fence altogether about the puppy prospect. "It's in God's hands," I said. "If it's meant to be, it'll be."

I went home and called the shelter.

A day later, the shelter proprietor, Barbara, called me back. "You're interested in Zane? I'm holding him for you. See you Saturday."

Gulp. What had I done? And how did I get through to her *this* time? Now I was in for it. I felt like a prank caller who'd been caught by his parents, or like Berger at the end of *Hair*, the movie. The guy played an innocent little prank to help out a friend in need and he gets shipped off to Vietnam for real.

A dog. Oh God, a dog. On top of that, Barbara's shelter was out in Jersey. I don't have a car. My head spinning, and not feeling at *all* sure of myself, I set the wheels in motion to try and procure travel arrangements for this unsettling adventure.

My default transport team, a friend who lives in Jersey, and a dog lover in the city with a car, were both unavailable that day. Was this my reprieve? Well, I'd tried. I even looked into public transportation, which turned out not to be an option. I said a prayer that "the perfect person at the perfect time and in the perfect way make him or herself available to me" if this dog was meant to be.

Right before I went to bed that night, a friend's name popped into my head. Kristen. A midwife. She lives in Brooklyn. I've never asked her to drive me anywhere in our many years of friendship. I asked. She was free.

My nerves still frayed, I requested guidance and signs from Spirit to let me know I was doing the right thing. Several synchronistic things happened in the days leading up to my pilgrimage to potential puppy land. I found a brand new stuffed panda bear toy on the ground. Mimi, my dear, dead mini dachshund, would have loved it. In fact, her favorite stuffed animal was a black and white cow, which mirrored her own colors. This panda looked an awful lot like Mimi's cow. A sign.

Next, while trolling the pet section of TJ Maxx (an old pastime with Mimi, who amassed a massive toy collection from their aisles) I came upon a Snoopy water bowl. Now, I was a Snoopy freak as a child, and I remain a fan today. Mimi even reminded me of Snoopy, and while I was walking her on a very depressing day, I found a Snoopy toy on the sidewalk. It wasn't any old Snoopy toy. It was Snoopy at the typewriter ("It was a dark and stormy night…"). This was delightful and much needed encouragement from Spirit to cheer me on with my writing before I was published.

I've never seen anything Snoopy at TJ Maxx, so I heeded the "sign," grabbed the water bowl and went on my way. It was a clear portent regarding the new dog from my old dog. Messages continued to pour in on the psychic "ticker tape." Harry Nilsson (John Lennon's favorite singer/songwriter)'s sweet and heartfelt "The Puppy Song" popped up on my iPod in shuffle mode. The morning of my trek to Jersey I found a tarot card laying on the floor from one of the five decks I pull cards from daily. How did it get there? Most likely, one of my cats knocked it down. Fine. But out of roughly two hundred fifty cards, *one* card lay face up on the ground. "You are on the Right Path."

I actually started to relax a little. As I ate breakfast, another beloved Harry Nilsson song, "Me and My Arrow" (about a boy and his dog from Nilsson's score for the animated children's film *The Point,* narrated by Ringo Starr) played on my iPod shuffle. The steady stream of signs was unmistakable. All systems were go.

Then there was that dream I had. I'd dreamt about Mimi a couple of times, and it was always amazing, hyper-real, and so rapturous to see, feel, and interact with my bosom buddy again. Now, dreams can mean lots of things. They can be a subconscious digesting of your day's activities. They can be precognitive. They can be "lucid" in that you have some incredible insight into your own life, consciousness, or spiritual development. You can have real time interactions with loved ones in spirit, or the spirits of those still in the flesh. For those who have had this powerful, visceral contact, you know it's not "just a dream." Every time I dreamt of Mimi, it had that hyper-real, palpable sense of a joyous reunion.

One night, months ago, I had a very strange dream about her. I stopped, dumbfounded, when I saw her facing me in suspended animation, frozen in mid-air, her posterior hovering over my window sill which is filled with potted plants. The bulk of her torso was levitating in

BRILLIANCE BREWING

a trotting position. She was neither dead nor alive, simply frozen in time. Astonished, I spoke her name. Thrilled to see her, albeit under such strange circumstances, I reached out slowly to touch her. As my hand approached her body, she began to unfreeze and come back to life, much like Sleeping Beauty or Snow White after the Prince's kiss.

This dream stuck powerfully with me, and I can still remember it like it was ten minutes ago. One of my friends said, "You had contact with her."

Yeah, I got that part, but I couldn't discern the unique aspects that were compelling me to analyze the dream's significance. The circumstances were too specific and macabre not to be more meaningful than simple contact.

I came up with this. I have a green thumb. So did my mom. I have brought many a plant back from the brink of death, near-lifeless plants my neighbors have thrown out in the trash room. I embrace and nourish them, and lo and behold, in a short time, the "goners" return and flourish. I'm that good. My window sill is a lush green healing zone.

"I bring things back from the dead," I thought. "I have the power of regeneration."

Mimi was suspended on my shelf of sunlight and greenery, the recovery room for resurrected plants, when I touched her. My touch is magic; I have the power to summon forth life.

That's what it meant.

I believe this is a latent power within all of us, to create, to renew, refresh, resurrect, and refurbish, starting with ourselves. "All this and more ye can do," said Jesus. That's what he was talking about. This may perhaps sound a bit grandiose to you but I can only reply that you haven't seen my plants.

When I considered that little Zane might be my Mimi come back to me, I got seriously choked up. I had asked her to come back, begged her when she was dying not to die, but if she did, I compelled her to return. I kept all her personal effects, her toys, her doggie bones, her beds, sweaters, and coats. It was now December Twentieth, five days before the holiday. Could she be coming home for Christmas? It was a most moving, magnificent, and miraculous prospect.

On that cold, damp and gray December morning I made the trek via bus and subway to Brooklyn. Every connection pulled in just as I arrived, a seamlessly choreographed commute. We picked up Kris's car from the shop then drove through the Isle of Staten to Nouveau Jersé.

We entered the adoption site, and I spotted Zane immediately. Like many other prospective men on the Internet, little Zane had misrepresented himself. Far from the tiny picture perfect photo that made him look like a star from *Sesame Street*, the real Zane had escaped from the set of *21 Jump Street*. He was a large, obstreperous teenage offender who barked loudly and incessantly the whole time Kristen and I were there. He was all grown up, on his hind legs, demanding attention.

It became obvious that "Zane" was short for "ZA-NY," a clear euphemism for crazy. He was not alone in his demented demeanor. There was another dog that stopped spinning in endless circles only long enough to poop and bolt it down lickety-split. It felt a bit like a doggie insane asylum. I've never backed out on a blind Internet date (though someone once did it to me, thanks guy!) but I whispered to Kristen, "Don't let her know it's us!"

I mean, the lady couldn't *make* me adopt him, but she had put him on hold for me, after not responding to my applications for other pups. Now I knew why. She couldn't wait to unload him.

Kristen was very chill about the whole thing, and while not pressuring me, she pointed out another dachshund since we were there. Sweet but skittish, she wasn't really "my type," and she was spoken for anyway. Her "intendeds" came to adopt her. Good.

We glanced at another of the three or four puppy playpens set up and Kris observed, "You don't need to look there." She comes from a family of Big Dog Lovers, a legacy of Old English Sheepdogs, Bassett Hounds, and currently an English bulldog. The rag tag gang here was small and scruffy looking. The yappy-dog type. Though no one was yapping.

I sighed and resolved to leave this unappealing situation, silently relieved. I told the ring-leader that I was sorry, but Zane was just too big and loud for my apartment, so I couldn't adopt him. To my relief, she took it all in stride. She'd allowed me to play with the spoken-for doxie, with the caveat that she was likely going to be adopted. She even called the potential adopters to see if they were still coming. But the point was, she was trying to work with me and I appreciated that.

"Can I just show you one dog before you go?" she offered.

"Sure" I replied. I'd humor her, convinced it would be another no-go. She walked us over to the small scruffy set.

"There's this little guy, Brando. He didn't look like much when he came in, but he's got personality."

He didn't look like much now—a tiny, scrappy, black and white feller. He was surrendered by his original owner, a lady truck driver. This I liked; the incongruity of a tough broad with this miniscule critter, and the absurdity of giving him such a macho name. What about this diminutive dog said muscle shirt and "I coulda' been a contender"?

He was barely three pounds and I could just see the two of them in the front seat of her truck while she smoked, cursed, and drank diet soda on the Jersey Turnpike. But the front seat of a truck is no place to raise a baby. At least she saw the error of her ways and surrendered him.

His hair was a mess and his eyes were both covered with gunk. I couldn't tell if he had cataracts or not, and wondered if he was, in fact, a tiny old man. Barbara assured me that he was a baby and directed me to look at his teeth. He was definitely a plebe.

Barbara encouraged us to take him down aisle four (the adoption event was held in a giant pet shop) and play. Kris and I sat on the ground and tried to bond with him. I didn't. She did. She held him in her arms like a baby. I tried it. Nothing happened. We tried to engage him with a toy (Barbara came prepared with accoutrements to entice). He wasn't interested. Neither was I. His hair was a mess. He didn't seem like much to me, or to like me much. He was just a dog. I looked away from him.

"I don't need a dog," I said aloud, stating the obvious. I didn't have to take any old dog. I didn't want a dog. I wanted *my* dog. I was crazy even to be here. I had had a very special dog, and no one here was special.

Kris picked him back up. "This is your dog."

I looked at her skeptically. "Why is he my dog?"

"Well, look how calm he is. He's not struggling to get out of my arms. Clearly, he wants to be where the action is with the other dogs, but he's not whining."

When we put him down he pattered off to be with the canine crowd, until we wrangled all three pounds of him back to aisle four.

"I don't need a dog," I repeated like a mantra. I was not convinced.

"Let's go get lunch. Think about it," Kris suggested.

What a great idea. What a great friend. She was the perfect person to go with, just as I had prayed for. I was in no position to make this decision, and frankly, I wasn't inclined toward adopting him. We explained our departure to Barbara and told her we'd be back in an hour.

Kris had just become a vegetarian, and I like healthy food. We drove around a bit, looking for the Thai restaurant Barbara mentioned but couldn't find it. We were surrounded by strip mall pizza parlors, delis and bad Chinese. Neither of us wanted this crap. With the pressure off, and the shift of scenery to relieve my stress, my mind cleared.

I was going to get the dog. It seemed capricious, probably crazy, but I just went for it. Acted from my gut, if not from my heart, because my heart was not yet in it. How could it be? I didn't know the little tyke yet.

We drove back and I adopted him. As I held the three month-old, three-pound pup in the front seat of the car I told Kristen the midwife, "You didn't deliver my baby, but you delivered me *to* my baby. Thank you."

This dog is not only perfect for me in every way, shape and form, he is my dog. I mean really, he is *my* dog. He's my little Mimi come back to me. I believe in reincarnation, and he is proof positive of the phenomenon (not that anyone else gets it, but it's my belief, my book, my life, and my dog). I've named him Milo after the little boy in *The Phantom Tollbooth* by Norton Juster, one of my favorite "kids" books with enough profundity to enlighten the most jaded of adults. Mimi had morphed into Milo. No doubt about it.

I went to Jersey to get Zane, a brown and black dachshund and came back with a black and white fluff ball. Mimi was black and white. Milo's black markings are *exactly* where Mimi's were. Are the personalities identical? Of course not. They're not supposed to be. What's the point of coming back and doing it *exactly* the same way? That's not how reincarnation works. We switch from male to female, rich to poor, warrior to monk, black to brown to white, red, and yellow, dachshund to Yorkie-Poo. We're here to experience variety. To learn from the past and improve upon it, take what we know and build on it.

We bring back markers, often scars (if you're human), as subconscious reminders of where we've been (a broken neck in a past life can manifest as neck pain in this life, a spear through the chest can result in a birthmark on the site of that mortal wound). Milo has recreated a little hop, an Irish jig in the right rear that Mimi had. He sits in Mimi's exact same spots in my home. He's silent like Mimi was, though he does growl at people in my hallway, which I sometimes enjoy (my "defender" is an animated cotton ball). He is calm and easygoing in public. No one knows he's with me if he's in a bag. Just like Mimi. He's stealth.

Everything that was wrong with Mimi is right with Milo. She was deformed, arthritic, and dense. He's perfectly healthy and light as a feather, like a balsa wood model plane. He's Mimi 2.0, the latest OS with improved hardware. He races down the hall like Mimi did, but now with no crippling consequences. Her engineering issues have been resolved.

Interestingly, Mimi humped more than Milo. Her stuffed cow toy was a favorite objet d'amour, and she tried to hump me once or twice, but I'm not gay and didn't go for it. Actually, Milo doesn't hump at all.

Mimi, while only five years-old, had a compromised body and wanted out. How could I stop her? In fact, when the time came, I offered an assist (via my vet). Just like Lily Von Schtupp in *Blazing Saddles*, who murmured, "Excuse me while I slip into something more...*comfortable*," Mimi exited the scene and did a quick costume change. Her Ford Model-T was weighing her down. She needed to streamline. Now she's an aerodynamic Ultra Light aircraft. The earthbound Dodo became a sparrow. It's almost hard to keep Milo grounded. He dances like a balloon, bouncing up and down the road in the wind.

I don't think any of my friends see it as I do. They probably think I'm crazy again (what's new?), but I've got the inside scoop. Keeping track of my psychic, spiritual, mental, and emotional data is my domain. Don't let anyone think they know more about you than you do.

Milo is not a hound, as Mimi was, which means his sense of smell is not as acute, nor is he OBSESSED with food the way Mimi was. She was a virtual gourmand from day one, delicately pulling the flesh off of her very first artichoke leaf without my having to explain it to her, and sharing mid-night nibbles of grapefruit with me. She was a food genius. She was also a little overweight, which didn't help her arthritis or deformities any. But how could I deprive her of one of her greatest joys in life, when it was also one of mine? She lived hard and ate fast.

When she was a pup she performed a magic trick while I was out. She got hold of a sealed plastic canister of freeze-dried chicken liver cat treats. She worked her puppy teeth like a can opener around the edge of the lid. It was precision cut, as if done by machine. She ate the entire jar (perhaps five ounces dry, but the equivalent of five pounds of chicken livers before they were freeze dried). She was fine, if full, but even more baffling was the fact that her gums were not bloodied or cut. She was born to eat well. And often.

At fifteen pounds, this made it difficult to carry her. And since she was deformed and arthritic, I had to carry her a lot as she was in pain. She would look up at me and I'd know it was time to hoist her in my arms or put her in her bag. While I'm used to carrying heavy loads since youth (tons of schoolbooks) and my purse probably weighs fifteen pounds anyway, it was frustrating to have that extra load when I wished I could just be out lightheartedly walking my dog. I wished she could exercise more, and so did she. She ran like the wind and loved to play, but it always took a toll on her. It was not only her weight. She developed deformities and severe limping shortly after I got her at eight weeks. Mimi's joie de vivre (and mine) was cut off at the knees.

I'm quite thrown by the fact that she's a boy now. The landscape has changed. I want to give her a belly rub, and I have to be careful not to deliver a hand job. But there it is. She's a boy. When I catch him out of the corner of my eye, or even see him in photos, I see Mimi. Tiny, black and white. The light in his brown eyes is the same. The relationship between us is identical. Not all the details, per se, but the energy of it, the pure adoration and joy we take in each other. The simpatico is still there. We're like Oblio, the boy and his dog in the song "Me And My Arrow." Right back where we started, but with a new lease on life. Mimi finally got a healthy body, just like in the song, "Everything Old is New Again" by Peter Allen. And I'm in a better place in every way than when I got her the first time. To be honest, I had been a bit crippled, myself.

After the extreme grieving I did after Mimi died, I blinked my eyes, and fifteen (miserable) months later, on a cold, dark day in December, the dog of my dreams came back to me. I am grateful every day.

As well, my dead tabby cat Wilbur has most assuredly returned as new silver tabby Celeste, and Mimi and Wilbur have simply picked up where they left off as best buddies, now masquerading as Milo and Celeste, running around the house and incessantly chewing on each other's ears, tails, and feet.

I don't know what to call any of them, frankly, and frequently default to "hey, you" after trying all the wrong (dead) names.

Wilbur and Mimi used to nap together, giant Wilbur would spoon from behind, his arm protectively around her. When Wilbur died, Mimi howled over his body. She was devastated.

She couldn't have cared less about my other cat, Angela, dead or alive.

For those who don't believe in reincarnation, I'm not trying to convince you. For those who know it to be true, the evidence is astounding.

After the deepest of depressions (I've had several over the decades), I am now in seventh heaven. It is Christmas, Easter, and the Fourth of July every day. This is how it works, we come, we go, then we come again.

I worked long and hard on myself while alone. I dredged myself out of a swamp. I, not Mimi, returned from the Underworld. She just came back from the body shop.

While crossing the street. I bumped into Jose, a favorite neighborhood doorman of mine. Character that he is, he's been quoted in my books before.

"How are you, honey?" He knew Mimi had passed.

"I got a new pup! I believe in reincarnation, and I really think he's Mimi. Except she's got a dick now!"

Never at a loss for a comeback, Jose jumped right in, "Chicks with dicks? Sure. I've seen 'em before."

Look up "The Puppy Song" by Harry Nilsson on

Youtube or iTunes. And look up the story of a little white boy named Luke who remembers being a black woman named Pam in his last lifetime. And also, "Supernatural Investigation" on Youtube, the story of James Linegar, a two-year-old boy from Louisiana who remembered being a pilot during WWII who was shot down near Iwo Jima. He remembers his name, the name of his buddy, the name of his aircraft carrier, all of which was verified.

CHAPTER 7

On Being Happy

I was on a leisurely mission to locate coconut oil in Whole Foods when, out of nowhere, a young mom barreled toward me like Cruella Deville swerving in her roadster.

With crazed eyes, her curly hair bouncing, she pushed a stroller containing her tiny newborn ahead of her and dragged a rolling grocery cart behind. I jumped out of her way as quickly as possible, veering left into the sushi section, when she crashed her baby into my cart as if we were bumper cars.

She stopped, her jaw agape, her eyes slit accusingly, as if I had done this thing to her. Rather, to her newborn.

She, like many new moms and nannies in crowded New York City, feel they always have the right of way because of their precious cargo and that we must all obediently back up to accommodate them, as I just had. It's the same principle as with the "Baby On Board" signs in cars. "You be careful now, our baby's special! Go ahead and crash into other people. We don't care about them."

I remained motionless and unrepentant as I stared staunchly at Bumper Car Mom. I would not accept liability when she was the one driving the vehicle out of control. Where were the Grocery Cops?

When I crept over to check out minutes later, there she was. I wanted to avoid her since I figured she would mouth off. My desire not to be yelled at notwithstanding, she was in the shortest line, so I bucked up and parked behind her, careful to keep back 200 feet (not hard with her sandwiched in between the baby stroller and shopping cart). She was so preoccupied with her smart phone that she discerned neither my presence nor the electronic notice to advance to the cashier. Since she missed her turn someone offered her their spot and she jumped at it, leaving her baby near the middle of the bustling central aisle, while her food cart was safely tucked in by the cashier.

This was a young woman with no self-awareness, and seemingly no real regard for her newborn. She expected me to have more concern for her infant than she did. This is something I, too, have been guilty of, expecting people to treat me better than I treated myself. People take their cue from you.

Sometimes, I have too much self-awareness, or perhaps I'm just too self-conscious. Regardless, I put my introspection to good use. As a student of Self, I analyze Me intently and scrupulously so that I work better next time. I'm now going to evaluate the recent ups and downs of my emotional chart so you can see how I expertly navigate my twists and turns of mood.

I started out having a great day. I went to a dance-centric exercise class with great music then bounced off to treat myself to a little beauty indulgence, eyelash extensions. I'm blonde on one half of my face—one set of lashes and the brow are pale blonde—and I have natural blonde streaks on that side of my head. If I'm not wearing makeup, I look really washed out. On one half of my face.

I had extensions put on once before, compliments of a friend. We went to an exclusive esthetician, one who caters to the Park and Fifth Avenue set. The extensions looked good but they were too long (they were "one size fit someone else") and they knocked into my sunglasses. It was weird having camel sized lashes, and it was odd having to work around the new appendages when taking makeup off. The filaments were dust traps. Still, they gave my eyes a certain definition. I started noticing that everyone in the old movies wore fake lashes. It makes the eyes "pop."

But the glue irritated my eyes when the extensions were applied, and, that, coupled with the jumbo lash size, made this a treatment I was not going to repeat. So I went back to my old washed-out, makeup-free look when I wasn't wearing makeup, which is often.

With spring in the air, I decided to do a little sprucing up. I got tired of looking at my washed out eye. When I wear makeup, it is a dramatically different look. So, I went to another salon, one I'd known about for a while, and was curious to try. The online reviews were great, and I took the plunge. I always say little prayers for "the most benevolent outcome" whether it's for lashes or lunch. It always works. I got a lovely young lady whose demeanor and glue were so gentle I almost fell asleep during the lengthy procedure (the lashes are attached one at a time). Already relaxed, the hand and foot massage took me over the top. And the lashes were perfect. They were Valerie size, not drag queen size.

It was lunchtime by the time my new glam set was glued on. I had a fruit and nut bar with me and was gifted with a can of Illy iced coffee from a promotional event on the street.

I was in the Flatiron district, right by Madison Square Park. The magic continued as I walked in. The park had a gorgeous new sculptural installation that looked like silver trees hovering from above.

It was a beautiful day, and I walked all the way home. I stopped in an old church, and dropped by Scandinavia House, whose clean design and colorful products always cheer me up. I popped into a nearby hotel gift shop and bantered with the classy Italian lady who runs it. We chatted amiably about several topics, including food and motorcycles, but I edged back a few inches when she turned vigorously anti-Semitic out of nowhere.

"And the Jews! How can the Jews claim to be organic? It's just a lie to make more money!"

First off, I wanted to tell her, they're usually going for the kosher thing, not the organic thing. Though there are organic-kosher venues. I had no idea what she was ranting about, but after she'd shocked me with a few more "Jews," I realized she'd been saying "juice" all along with her Italian accent. So, she was only slandering the organic producers whom I support (and am well aware that there are pretenders among them, but certainly not all of them). From there, I walked into Grand Central Terminal and was offered another promotional product, a peach popsicle (not organic, or kosher, though I asked). While strolling through the palatial space, I bumped into a friend.

This was a breezy, "free" flowing day, one of unexpected pleasures.

In the past, the lashes, sweet coffee, and frozen treat were all little indulgences I would have denied myself. However, by accepting them, I was getting happier and happier by the minute. I was *flowing* with life, or was "in the Vortex," according to the teachings of channel Esther Hicks and non-physical "consciousness" Abraham.

I got home, grabbed my pooch, and went for a jaunty walk. It was a hot day, so I gravitated toward shade and sought the breeze from the river. Everything was flowing magnificently. Though they were all the simplest of pleasures, a day filled with tiny treats adds up to a jackpot.

Until...

Until I saw someone I don't like. A crazy neighborhood broad I was familiar with from my walks with my last dog. She'd coo over your dog then tell you how to walk it, what to do with it, what you were doing wrong. I'd heard her scream at people. I learned to avoid her, at all costs. I'd been on the lookout for her with my new pooch, keen to protect us both from her poisonous energy. I sidestepped a redhead who looks a lot like her, but it wasn't her. I remained vigilant, watching out for the crazy carrot top.

By the time I got close to the real one and turned tail to avoid her, she'd spotted me and started cooing over my new dog like a witch cackling over her brew. She shouted after me, "Oh, what a *cute* little puppy! Can I say *hello*?"

I could have ignored her and kept walking, but that's not what I did.

The "nice" (stupid, guilty, people-pleasing) part of me turned back to grant her wish. She did nothing crazy and said all the right things. She patted my dog, though he kept his distance from her. But I had gone against myself. I gave priority to her desire over mine. I turned the rest of my afternoon to crap. Do you see what I just wrote? She didn't ruin my day. *I did.* I took a great mood and turned it to mud.

I was mad at myself. Why didn't I just keep going and ignore her request? I don't owe her a thing, not my time, my company, nor the right to touch my dog. This happens frequently with dogs, as with babies. How do parents deal with this? You don't want anyone and everyone touching your baby. I don't want everyone touching my dog, including other dogs. You have to be protective by being selective.

What was so remarkable was how quickly I let my happiness fly out the window—hell, I practically hurled it. The peach-popsicle-iced-coffee-jubilee was centuries ago on a continent far away. I berated myself. "Why did you stop for her? Why did you give her what she wanted? Why were you (horror of horrors) *nice*?" I don't believe in being nice. I believe in being true to myself. "Nice" is to appease others. Being true to yourself is an act of power that ultimately benefits everyone.

She was not welcome in my life, but I tolerated her in the name of social propriety. And this I did for a woman who screams like a raving maniac on the sidewalk. I tried to rationalize it. Maybe we helped her? I know my dog is a healer, and so am I. But that angle didn't work because that was not my intention in stopping. It was to "be polite" to someone who is not at all polite. That's what galled me about my behavior. I don't turn the other cheek to people who treat me badly. I avoid them (if they're strangers), or confront them (if they're not).

I finally realized that I had to forgive myself and reframe the interaction. Okay, so I don't want further interactions with her. I won't answer her call the next time. I'm not her dog.

I was starting to feel better, but I wasn't out of the woods yet. This was a particularly bothersome issue because it's been a pattern of mine in the past—being "nice" and doing things that I didn't want to do, even something as simple as answering an invasive question. Because someone asks you a question does not mean you are obligated to answer. I'm still learning that one. It's my "good girl" upbringing that makes answering and being "nice" (a despicable behavior) a knee jerk reaction at times. One I take responsibility for. It's not my jerky knee's fault. Nor is it my parents'. Who I was raised to be was then. Who I choose to be is now.

To give myself yet more peace I made up this story: This encounter with the witchy maniac was pre-destined. She'd been on my mind, and well, now, it's over with. I know she has short hair now. I'm attuned to her frequency. I do not have to humor her any more than I had to apologize to the young mom who crashed into me with her baby in the supermarket. In fact, I should have sued *her* for bruising my groceries. It's all about taking care of myself, being *my* best friend and biggest advocate. If you're not for you, how can you expect others to be?

This is my spirituality. Some people may view it as selfish, but it ain't. It's about loving myself. Protecting myself. And my dog. When people are happy and fulfilled they are genuinely nicer and more giving. It's then that they can easily afford to be what appears to be "selfless," but is, in fact, truly Self Full. When you're fully in your Big Self, you are brimming with love, joy, and bonhomie. Enough for all.

But not until your cup is full. And yes, "full cup" is open to interpretation. It doesn't mean you need *everything* on your wish list, for those are just things, and "things" (even jobs and marriages) do not make you happy. *You* make you happy. Your attitude. Your beliefs. Your behavior. Only, *ever*, do what you want to do. This includes taking out the trash. Of course you want to take it out, just as you want to pay your taxes. You know what the consequences are if you don't.

Wanting covers a broad spectrum, and we define it variously at different times. But don't blame your obligations and choices on others. We all have reasons for doing the things we choose to do. Take responsibility for who you are and what you do. It's empowering to do so.

I eventually stopped tormenting myself, but not before I slipped on a dog bone in my apartment and went flying, banana peel style, and landed on my bad knee. Not the one I recently had surgery on. No, that's my *good* knee now. My other knee decided it was jealous of all the attention the other knee got and has been tight and profoundly painful to bend. I don't know what's wrong with it, exactly, but it's problematic for someone who likes to exercise. I landed on the kneecap and screamed. My cats stared at me. My dog licked my toe.

This is a perfect example of how the law of attraction works. When you feel good, you attract peach popsicles and iced coffee. When you feel bad, you attract crap. At least I didn't land on it.

Which leads me to another story.

When my puppy was being toilet trained to go on newspaper, he made occasional mistakes, as all puppies do. Unbeknownst to me, I stepped in some "misplaced" poo, tracking it on a dark carpet all the way to the kitchen. By the time I figured out what was going on, I had to clean my poopy shoe (which had deep rubber treads), the floor, the carpet, and my dirty, cursing mouth out with soap.

The next day, I heard a thunderous crash-bang and searched my apartment to locate the source of the impact. One of my plants (with a long, mane-like mass of leaves) was on the floor. This plant has been tormented for *years* by various felines in my home. This day, the mane was decapitated from the stalk by a young, feline perpetrator. It was an herbal crime scene. Soil was everywhere.

The puppy had just peed on the clean bedding in his crate (boo, hiss!) and his feet were soaking in urine, so I threw him into the kitchen sink for a bath. After drying him off, I caught him sniffing around the rest of the plant soil I had not yet cleaned up. My dog is mostly white so this would not do. I scooped him up out of the danger zone then rushed through the kitchen, where I promptly slipped on the floor, wet from his bath, nearly killing both of us and potentially wrecking my (then) newly operated-on bad knee (which is now my good knee). A finger was smashed in the melee. It hurt like a mother, swelled, and turned purple.

I whipped out the vacuum cleaner. The dog, floor, and dog crate were now clean. I held services for the houseplant as I glowered at the cat. The only thing that was still filthy was me.

The next morning, Milo pooped on the rug again. While carrying the poop, I tripped on a box in my hallway and fell. The poop went flying. Okay, kind of hilarious, kind of embarrassing, kind of appalling, given what I was carrying. Had I fallen on the poop? I looked cautiously underneath me. Some of it was still in hand (wrapped in a paper towel) and some of it had scattered. But none of it was under me, thank goodness.

What's my point in telling you all this? When you're "on a roll," it can swing either way. Peach popsicles. Or flying crap. The skies can darken or brighten in a second. Just don't forget you're navigating the ship. You can turn it around with your thoughts, which then create your feelings.

Your point of attraction is what you are thinking and feeling. When your predominant vibration is one of peace and happiness, things flow smoothly and easily for you, as they're intended to. Life is supposed to be easy. Life is supposed to be fun. The best way to enjoy it is by not getting in your own way (with negative thoughts and beliefs). If you don't want to believe that, then continue on as you were. It's a free country. But for those who feel the joy in that liberating sentiment, continue on with me.

Nothing stays the same. We are continuously being born anew. Wise people take advantage of that fact and live in the moment, recreating themselves guided by their ever-evolving desires. (Have you considered that the term "recreation," comes from re-creating?) People who say "same shit, different day" (I know several of these, they're *tons* of fun) literally recreate the same shit every day. They star in the world's longest running (boring) play. Their life is purgatory. They have no idea that they have created their prison sentence based on their beliefs. They paint the same picture every day based on their expectations and behaviors.

Ours is a world of chiaroscuro, light defined by dark, a world of contrast that offers infinite and ever-changing choices. If you're not happy, choose again. The word repent comes from the French for re-think (penser). Think again. Pick a new color palette and repaint. Game over? Play again. And again. And again. World without end.

If you recall in *Ground Hog Day* (one of my favorite movies), Bill Murray's character recreates the same crap day in, day out, until he has epiphanies that change his attitude from one of grumpiness to gratitude, curiosity, and joy. He transforms his life. And, yes, eventually, he gets the girl. What he had to do first was to choose love and appreciation of self as he learned to play piano, save lives, get degrees, goof around. When Bill's character started having fun, playing and engaging with life instead of resisting and resenting it, his dream (getting the girl) came true. *Enjoying himself was the more important gift that then enabled the second.*

When you feel good, good things happen. And don't argue with me that bad things can happen when you're feeling good. I know that. I live here. What I'm asserting is that we live in an ever shifting wave form universe. Water flows around the boulder in the stream. If you want to try to move the boulder, or sit stranded on it, that's your business. We are energy, vibration. Take advantage of that fact and go with the FLOW instead of staying static, or, worse yet, trying to swim upstream. If something puts a cramp in your style, dust yourself off and get moving in a different direction. Don't waste time bitching about it. There are plenty of things that *are* out of our control. When you accept that, you liberate yourself. Save your energy to work on your attitude, not save the world. Adding a sane, healthy person to the planetary roster ultimately helps everyone.

When you consistently raise your vibration to one of love, joy and appreciation, you consistently and increasingly create things that will please you. We are spawn of the Great Pooh Bah in the Sky, and we are created in Her Fantabulous Image. Life is an ever flowing, ever-expanding wave of curiosity, wonder and creation. When we achieve balance we not only surmount the vicissitudes of life but expertly surf the waves.

If something has happened which displeases you, you are well within your rights to be disappointed. Nothing is worse than being encouraged by others to put things into perspective, to "buck up, things will get better" when things are not yet better. That's forcing the issue. We need to feel what we are feeling until we're ready to process it. Go ahead, sulk, mope, cry, do what you need to do, just don't take it out on others. Excuse yourself from the room. Take a time out. No one wants to vomit in public. You need a bathroom to sort things out. You can't escape the black cloud you're sitting under without understanding it. After all, you created it. The point is to get the message from it. It's your message to yourself, using the symbolism and imagery (dog poop, crazy lady) of the external world. The world is a projection of our minds. One could even consider the black cloud's message to be a gift with the potential to transform you. As an amusing aside, as I was reviewing this sentence, I just got an email with some "bad" news pertaining to a glitch in one of my audio books that was about to go on sale. I had to review several audio files and compare them to the text in a non-fiction book that was very complicated and revise one of the files. I kept my anxiety at bay, focused intently, and resolved the situation quickly. Nothing like a little show and tell.

Now, the "something disappointing" which happened may seem to be the cause of your unhappiness, but I'm going to challenge you on this. An event is simply that. A happening. Neither good nor bad. It is your judgment about the thing that creates either your discomfort or elation.

Don't get testy and say that some things are unequivocally bad (such as a bomb blowing your legs off). For the sake of this argument, everything will remain a neutral "event." Something exploded. There was pain, fear, blood, and some rearranging of your anatomy. You weigh less. That's a factual description of circumstance free of judgment, a skill that will serve you well if you learn to analyze things thusly. It can help you to step back and look at things this way, even extreme things, as a counterpoint to the part of you that is embroiled in the drama, terror or pain. Maybe not in the middle of the event, but certainly after the fact as you're trying to piece yourself back together. Perspective makes the difference between whether you identify as a victim or a survivor, as someone who was "traumatized" or someone who has "lived." To live one's life feeling like a victim has profound consequences. It means you will keep attracting and creating circumstances which confirm your existence as a victim.

But I'm not talking about big explosions today, we're starting small. Please select a nice, manageable disappointment of your own to explore. All the little things (dog pee, dead plants, smashed fingers, and crushed kneecaps) can add up to one nice, big funk. If you're not mindful of your choices, you can start by simply missing a bus and end up having a crappy hour, day, week, or life.

From analyzing circumstances and my reactions to them, and making mental, emotional and behavioral changes, happiness is now my default state, not depression. It used to be the other way around. I used to think, "Why can't I just be happy like normal people?" As if "normal" exists.

People are intent on *appearing* happy. Many repress their true feelings and put on a show, or take lots of pills and get lots of plastic surgery to "save face." People go through the motions, doing what they think they should do (shag, marry, breed, acquire more money, higher status and the symbols that represent it). In our culture, if you're cute and young and rich you've got it made. For ten minutes. Cause you don't remain a larva for long. Old age sets in, fortunes change, and that's that. Everything in this world is ephemeral and ever changing. The sands always shift. That's something you can use to your advantage.

What had disconcerted me in the example I gave earlier was how quickly I went from feeling on top of the world (from my series of simple pleasures) to bottoming out. In fact, *I* shifted the sands that day by making a choice that went against myself, then compounded my discomfort by punishing myself for that decision (heck the crazy lady didn't scream at me, but I sure as heck did). I doubled my displeasure by judging myself harshly.

If you look at my interaction with the lady on the street (something I judged as terrible) what really happened? A woman talked to me and petted my dog. Now, I had my reasons for being upset about allowing that interaction, as I explained to you, whether or not you understand my beliefs regarding the interaction. It doesn't matter. What matters is that you understand *your* own process. If you don't have one, create one. Always be able to explain yourself to yourself.

When you accept what *is* (the dark and the light, the highs and the lows) you gain a loftier perspective. You become wise. You swerve skillfully around boulders in your path. Perhaps the boulders will even disappear. You can dance on top of them or swim around them. Laugh at them. Lunch on them.

You have options. This is the key: *how* you approach something changes the nature of it. A mountain becomes a molehill. You start to enjoy life instead of being traumatized by it.

Instead of chiding myself for doing (or not doing) something, I'm learning to move with my lows and learn from them, loving myself gently, just as if I were unwell. This way, I don't stay stuck and behave like a broken record obsessing over my perceived infractions (which are just my subjective judgments, anyway). What you resist, persists. What you embrace has the potential to transform. If you're not happy, simply *choose again.*

I view myself at times as a bird of prey gliding high above the landscape, riding the thermals, adjusting to shifts in pressure, temperature and atmosphere. The eagle sees everything big and small. It floats, soars, and dives. Sometimes it catches its prey. Sometimes it doesn't. It doesn't piss and moan when it misses. That would be conduct unbecoming an eagle.

Instead of assessing my highs as good and my lows as bad, I'm trying to develop a broader stance. One that embraces dualism so thoroughly that it allows me to transcend it and move into triality, the position above. That's the all-seeing Masonic eye on top of the pyramid.

It's not satanic. It's brilliant. It is a coveted spiritual position that seekers aspire to. To live in this world, but not of it. To remain stabilized throughout turbulence. Conquer your self and you conquer the world. Not oppressive dominance over the self or the world, but spiritual mastery incorporating the gentle embrace of the divine feminine (We've been living from an unbalanced patriarchal perspective for millennia). When you love and accept yourself, the highs, the lows, and everything in-between, miracles happen.

Happiness is our natural state of being. It is our "God Essence," from whence we issue, and it is ours to enjoy when we are receptive to it. Like a plane that cruises calmly over the clouds, we too can connect with that peaceful space, even when part of us, the part engaged in the world of light and shadow, is pretending to be sad, angry, or miserable.

It's all an act. An illusion as seemingly real as your dreams each night. At heart, we are all made of love. The rest is an act. The drama ends when we decide it does.

I saw the crazy red-headed lady again. We were crossing the street toward each other. She saw my dog and lit up, eager to catch us again in her witchy energetic web.

A car came between us and I walked around it, avoiding her entirely, as was my desire. Easy. Effortless. My stomach didn't tighten as I'd already made the decision not to interact with her. I knew what I wanted (no more crazy) and the car acted as God's proxy. As My proxy.

When you consistently connect with the part of your self that is above the fray (through prayer, solitude, meditation, making increasingly more comfortable choices) you can more easily navigate the drama of daily life. The nature of this world is polarity. Your True Nature is Unity. Keep your chin up, your eyes on the prize, and enjoy the ride.

CHAPTER 8

Building Peace

I was talking with a couple I had just met about one of my favorite new age speakers, Esther Hicks, who channels the energy of "Abraham" a collective consciousness. Just *thinking* about Esther and Abe puts me in a good mood. If I watch one of their DVDs, I beam pretty much from beginning to end during their lengthy programs, then float off on a cloud. The "vibration" they embody is what they teach, how to get happy, and from there, how to become even happier.

This couple loved Esther and Abe, too, and as we excitedly talked I started to share some of my personal story with them. The wife began arguing with me. About my life. Huh? This has happened before. Someone fails to understand what I am saying and then projects their own mishegas on me. What had started as a happy and inspired connection devolved into a tense assessment about my path, and I didn't appreciate her judgments.

I gave a brief synopsis of how I went from being lonely and depressed after losing my parents when young, feeling frustrated and sorry for myself after an early marriage ended in an early divorce, to the triumphant status I claim today, that of being mostly happy most of the time. This is a gargantuan, top of Mt. Everest accomplishment for me, of which I am most proud, particularly since I did it by myself. There's no one in my home cheering me on (though I do have marvelous friends). The loss of my nuclear family was my Achilles heel, producing a purgatory of pain over the decades.

My new acquaintance argued, "Have you heard nothing Abraham says? You are *never* alone. Spirit is always with you!"

I've heard this one before.

This gal was referring to the idea that we are surrounded by our loved ones in spirit. That God is around us. I believe that, too, but I don't always "feel" it. I'm human. I've lived with grief and deep depression and fought long and hard to replace those dark emotions with peace and joy. However, this woman lives with someone. Happily married. Her husband was right there with her. Shut up.

"I know all about life after death, but when they're dead, they're dead."

"But you're *not* alone, and they're not *really* dead," she persisted.

Harumph. I girded myself. "I am alone," I retorted. "I did not say that I am lonely, but I most certainly live alone, spirits or not!"

For the love of God, this was ridiculous. What the hell were we arguing about? We both believe in an afterlife, but I'm the one who's single with the dead parents. More importantly, she was telling me how to feel. When you're grieving, it's no comfort that your loved ones are still alive (somewhere else) or ever so close to you (when you can't see, feel, or hear them). With a good medium you can communicate with your loved ones, and after having such experiences myself, my grief really started to abate. Furthermore, I'm not grieving anymore. I was explaining to this couple where I *had* been, which makes my emotionally elevated status all the more significant.

I live alone but don't feel alone (for the most part), and there's the difference. Alone is not the same thing as lonely. You do not have to be loved to feel loved. We create feeling tones with our thoughts and beliefs. I have learned how to choose new thoughts that connect me to my loved ones in spirit. And I have new beliefs about life that make me feel good. As a result, I'm happier, and my connection to Spirit (including loved ones, and my Soul Self) is stronger. This woman was barking up the wrong tree, preaching to the choir and trying to out-philosophize a philosopher.

I'm as "out there" as they get when it comes to metaphysics, extra-terrestrials, ascension, enlightenment, multi-dimensionality, you name it, I'm on it. And while I know that our loved ones continue to live on after they leave the body, they do not continue to have breakfast with us. If my mother is talking to me, I don't hear her. She doesn't do the dishes. I do, however, get many signs from Spirit (some in the kitchen, so Hi, Mom!) And while this is amusing and reassuring, it is *not* the same as a flesh and blood relationship. How could it be? I'm the one with the dishpan hands.

I was agitated. She interrupted with commentary about my life when she didn't know me. I am proud of my solitary status, though I have wanted to and still do wish to be partnered with the right man at the right time. I had tried to describe to this couple my long journey from despair to my triumphal celebration of who and what I am today. My solitude has provided the platform from which I have derived both strength and wisdom. The fact was that I was quite happy that evening until she started contradicting me.

"I'm not complaining," I corrected her, "I'm *explaining*. And I never said I was lonely. I said I live alone."

When I worked for AIG, I regularly had lunch at a local Japanese restaurant.

The hostess greeted me, "How many?"

"Just one."

To which she countered slowly, each and every day, "*All* by yourself?"

I glowered. "Yes."

What's wrong with eating by yourself? I like it just fine. A lot of people are not confident enough to do it.

Back to the annoying wife. The husband interrupted, discerning my discomfort, and the fact that this conversation was not advancing harmoniously. He turned to her. "If you died tonight, I'd be upset."

"But I'd still be with you!"

"But not in our bed. Not in my life."

No body, no nookie. No breakfast. No vacuuming. No arguing. No marriage. Sorry. He understood my position.

It's a very difficult transition for the bereaved to go from earthy flesh and blood to airy "essence" of loved one. That is, if you're sensitive enough psychically and spiritually to pick up on their post-mortem vibration. Most people aren't. Most people are engaged full throttle in this fast, flashy, ADHD world. We are consumed with distraction. The ability to easily access peace and "presence" is not in most folks' skill set. When someone dies, even if they've been sick and fading for a long time, their departure from the body presents the bereaved with a cold turkey withdrawal from the warmth of flesh and the viability of their visage. You can get emotional D.T.s (delirium tremens, an alcoholic's shaking from lack of alcohol) from "loss of loved one." I had a bad case of it for years. The heaviness of grief also creates a wall that makes it *very* difficult for Spirit to penetrate in order to communicate with you. You don "cement shoes" and become incommunicado when you are inconsolable. It was hard work to pull out of my abyss. But I did it. And that's what I'm so darn proud of. That's what I was trying to tell this couple.

The wife went on to express her deep concern that Esther Hicks, whose husband of many decades died a few years ago, be paired up with someone new.

"Why?" I inquired. "It's relatively soon for her. And he was the love of her life. Why does she need to be coupled?"

Esther was back to doing the work they did joyously together as a couple, has a loyal support staff and worldwide audiences that adore her. It was quite impressive to me that she was carrying on without him.

"I just don't want her to be alone!"

Clearly, what was good for me (take comfort in your dead relatives, you're not *really* alone) was not good enough for Queen Esther. Which makes me think the gal is simply afraid to be alone herself. It's her issue, which is why she reacted so strongly to my declarations.

I didn't bother arguing Esther's case. In fact, Esther, despite whatever grieving process she did or continues to go through, has continued her professional life most magnificently. I'm impressed with how she is carrying on without her husband, who was also her business partner. She is an inspiration to me. We don't have to be downed by despair. We don't need to be coupled to be happy. We must find and create our own happiness and not rely on others to provide it for us. For as surely as they appear, people, and things, disappear. If you rely on props for your happiness "fix," you're a junkie as surely as an addict. Find the "fountain of youth" within, *your* source of joy, wisdom and peace, and you will always be okay, despite temporary setbacks. Indeed, you will be happy. That's enlightenment. You don't lose your humanity, your feelings, the experience of ups and downs per se, but you do gain tremendous inner strength. And as you scale higher levels of spiritual growth, one transcends even the highs and lows of duality. Personally, I'm getting there, and this was what I was trying to express to this couple. Instead of comprehending what I was getting at, the wife blurted out one final frustration.

"I just want everyone to be happy!"

Well now, how exactly does *that* work? I know this much, you can't help others unless you yourself are doing the work. Unless you are mostly happy, most of the time, and can figure out how you got there, only then is there the possibility of inspiring others to do the same. They will not replicate your results. We are on unique paths; our means to happiness will be different. We can certainly compare notes. But wanting it for them means nothing unless they want it themselves.

Wanting happiness for others is a quagmire. Sure, it's a nice idea and I'd like it too. Happy people are nice people. Happy people don't start wars. Happy people are loving. That's how it works, not the other way around. If someone is not loving, they are not happy. It's that simple. But you can't *make* others happy. The corollary, which is quite freeing, is that you can't make others unhappy either. Not many people believe this, but if one is true, then so is the other. The bottom line? We are all responsible for how we feel. Once we become accountable, the world changes. You are empowered. You wait for no one. You wait for nothing. Change the way you think, and your world transforms.

That's why personal happiness (and the pursuit of it) is so darn important and not selfish at all. It's the best thing you can do to help the world, and that's why it's in our Constitution. Help yourself. When your needs are truly met (however you define this) the love that bubbles up within you will naturally bubble out and spill over onto others. Their happiness compounds yours, and things just get better and better.

But to think that people do not have a right to be unhappy, or angry, or confused is not helpful. People are perfect exactly where they are. If they want to be angry, they have a right to be. If they want to be happier, and feel relief, they have a right to that, too. But to dictate compulsory happiness by forcing "happiness" directives on others is nonsense. You can't even *become* happier if you don't believe it's possible, or a worthy goal. Thoughts and beliefs are the basis of everything.

You can't bypass the process of transforming your moods. You must accept them as is, embrace them, and trust that there is a reason why you are feeling what you are feeling. Once you figure that out (ask yourself questions!) or if you're able to simply choose the better feeling thoughts which produce better feeling feelings (these are master skills), you can get there by yourself. But it's a *process*. The movement is incremental. You don't go directly from being miserable to being ecstatic. You have to move up the emotional scale feeling by feeling. This is done by dialoguing with yourself, figuring out what feels bad (it all starts with a thought, a belief, or a judgment about something) then choosing better feeling thoughts that empower and uplift you. Rinse and repeat.

Remember what I said earlier about nothing meaning anything? That an event is just that, a neutral experience, neither good nor bad, until we attach our judgments (beliefs) to them. While you might feel understandably furious (hurt, enraged, wounded...homicidal) if you discover your spouse has cheated on you (bad! bad!! BAD SPOUSE!!!) consider that there are very specific reasons why you are reacting to the event, based specifically on *your* beliefs. If someone were in a similar situation, their judgments and beliefs might overlap some with yours, but not entirely. Some people might not even care. Others might be glad (Good, now I can divorce her!) or relieved (Thank God, now *I* don't have to sleep with him) Everyone has different agendas.

For example, in questioning yourself regarding what's going on, here's an abbreviated, imaginary conversation:

"Why are you so mad?"

"Because he (or she, but I'm stopping with the he/she now) hurt me."

"How did he hurt you?"

"By betraying me!"

"What do you mean by betray?" (It's good to figure out how and why you're defining things, because everybody thinks differently. You are excavating, and, hopefully, renovating your mind.)

"He wasn't loyal!"

"How does his being disloyal hurt you?"

"It means he doesn't love me!"

"Why does it mean that?"

"Isn't it obvious? If he really loved me, why would he do that?"

"Why do you think?"

"'Cause he's a jerk. What other reason could there be? Maybe because he's mad at me? I've been working hard and haven't been as available to him as I used to be. You know, he did want to talk about our relationship a few months ago, but I kept pushing it off, afraid of what he would say. Maybe if I had talked with him, this wouldn't have happened."

(The seeker might start to cry. Anger has turned to doubt, remorse, and sadness, all based on new lines of thought. The mind produces emotions via thought.)

"Why are you crying?"

"Because this is just so sad! I really do love him, but I've been mad at him for not being understanding when I lost my job, and unsupportive when I was looking for a new one, so when I found a new job, I just threw myself into it and made *that* my new relationship. Things weren't feeling so good at home. They still aren't, but I can't stand to think of ending this relationship."

"Okay, so what are you thinking of now?"

"To talk with him, like he asked to before I lost my job, before I threw myself into my new job, and before he had this stupid affair. Oh, God, this *is* all my fault!"

"How is this all your fault?"

"Well, I didn't talk with him when he wanted to, but he wasn't sensitive when I lost my job, and he's the one who cheated! We both participated in creating this mess."

"What are you wanting now?"

"To chew him out! To tell him how hurt and angry I am that he went outside of our relationship to feel better, instead of reaching out to me. Oh right, he did try to reach out to me. Well, maybe he could have tried harder! I don't know what I think, or want. I'm very confused."

"What are you confused about?"

"Maybe I brought this whole thing on. Maybe I made him cheat!"

"How did you make him cheat?"

"Nobody makes you do anything. You can't *make* someone cheat. Okay, so I didn't make him cheat. He made that choice. But I've made choices, too. I guess we really have to talk."

This is a classic example of an autonomous Socratic dialogue. It implies that you have the answers to all your questions, right inside. You are your own best expert. Use the dialogue above (which I made up) to figure out the intricacies of the thought/belief/feeling system that works within all of us. It's a simple exploration of what's in your mind and heart. There's always room for some emotional Feng Shui.

The made up person above could continue to hate, be mad, want revenge, want to break up, or could expand her perception regarding what he did (and what she did as well) that led up to their current state of affairs. If she chooses to view her situation as awful, she will feel awful. It's fine if she does, and it's important to remember that. If, after dialoguing with herself, she can shift her perspective to—"I don't like this situation, but perhaps it will get better, maybe even bring us closer together. And if not, it may lead us to moving on to more fulfilling relationships. Or time alone? Maybe I really *do* want to focus on my job, and *not* a relationship at this time."—then she can feel better, with more clarity, even in the midst of the discord. When we judge something as bad, we create discomfort for ourselves. When we suspend judgment, we make space for new, possibly more forgiving experiences.

Do you see how through analysis it was possible to perceive different angles of the situation? What seemed "all bad" at first became softer and more mutable as thoughts and feelings were examined from a position of non-judgment. This is imperative. Don't judge yourself for judging, feeling bad, spiteful, petty, small or pathetic. When you accept your human nature, you can revision yourself (and others) in a more loving and empowered manner.

That being said, based on the example above, you are not required to love, forgive, or take back the mate who cheated on you (ignores you, beats you, blah blah blah). Being loving and spiritual does not mean you have to forgive and forget. In fact, being spiritual means nothing.

Decide what it means for *you*. But I urge you to put your thoughts and feelings first as you contemplate the broader perspective which encompasses others. Honor yourself. The kinder you are to yourself, the easier it is to be kind to others. Even as you divorce their ass.

If you really can't stand the guy (job, home, situation), come to terms with it as is, then take solid action to move toward situations that will feel better (more in alignment with who you are now and what you want). If you don't do the mental and emotional work to figure out how you got into a mess in the first place, however, you will end up in a similar mess again, and often in an even worse mess, as your Soul waits for you to figure out the lesson, not run away from it. Got it? Your Soul isn't trying to make things *harder*. It's trying to make things *clearer*. There is always a gift from each lesson learned.

Abraham (via Esther) teaches taking personal responsibility for our emotional states of being. In fact, Esther, from what I can discern, has chosen to embrace life, for now, as a single person. However, she's written that when she is happy and "vibrationally" high, she can *feel* her husband Jerry's energy clear as day. Happiness heals and it opens doors.

Last but not least, the woman I was talking with commented that writing is a lonely business and advised that one should always have a writing partner. This is a perfect example of a belief, not truth. I am as happy writing alone as I am living alone. In fact, I had a writing partner for many years, and it was one of the most challenging relationships I've ever had. Loneliness seemed to be a theme (or a fear) for my new acquaintance, and she was projecting it onto me.

How happy was this Pollyanna? I'm guessing that if she was less fearful and more confident, she wouldn't have jumped down my throat.

The bottom line was that although we both love Abraham and Esther, we were not on the same wavelength. Not even a little bit. Since I value my peace and happiness and it was going down the toilet talking with her, I made a hasty exit so I could start growing my happiness again. I wasn't going to convince her of anything (nor was I trying to) and she had not changed my mind about anything, either.

You can never truly understand another person. If you're lucky, you make strong and continued efforts to understand yourself. Nothing happens by default. *The thoughts you think and the beliefs you choose create your emotions and your experiences.* Make a study of yourself and how you work. You are a topic worthy of attention. Identify your triggers and examine the beliefs behind them. Be able to explain yourself to yourself at all times. There are no accidents. Your life is a finely tuned machine, you are the engineer, and your thoughts are your fuel. Put positive and empowering thoughts in your tank. Clean the tank when it's dirty. When you know this, you can start to direct your life in new, more fun and satisfying directions.

So, how do we build peace?

Thought by thought. Decision by decision.

When you prioritize your happiness and understand how truly important joy is to a successful life, you must question your choices. How does this *feel*? Do I *want* to do it? Arguably, there are things one "must" do, like earn a living, or cook your food, or take care of your kids. But if you're feeling put upon by such things, consider the alternative. No income, no food, no family. When it comes down to it, these are all things you *do* want. So, taking care of them is in alignment with your wants, even if there is a repetitive aspect of daily life that can seem tiresome. When you choose the empowered perspective, rather than feeling put upon, you can appreciate what you have and move in gratitude *with* your choices, not against them in resentment, and fill your days with grace.

How easily do you hold your peace? If you're like me, you can be having a great day, a wonderful morning, and something will happen that shatters your cool. For me, today, it was my kitten exploding into a very loud, hacking cough. This brought up fears concerning vet bills and death (I *just* got her, is she gonna die?). I just took my puppy to the vet yesterday for an ear infection, did I really have to go *right* back the next day? What was wrong with her? Instead of running to the vet, I did some online research then called my de facto cat expert, a pal who has many (*many*) cats. He has several with asthma and he explained how he deals with it. It made sense to me. While I am still on edge (as is my cat, utterly confused by this new, rattling development), I am taking a wait and see approach. I'm also giving her an herbal lung support liquid that I had from another cat. Taking action is key when there's an issue. If I need to take her to the doctor, I will, but I didn't have to do so today. Sometimes things work themselves out.

I was already feeling a little uneasy today (this was not one of those relaxed, happy mornings), so the feline turn of events was right in line with my mood. I was worrying about the future, a nice, diffuse topic. Since I understand how the law of attraction works, I knew my nerves and my kitten's cough were both in alignment with fear. It was my job to reverse that for both of us.

Celeste is the feline equivalent of Dennis the Menace. I'm frequently mad at her for upending my house. Lately, I've felt like the angry mother of a recalcitrant teenager. Her illness made me realize I've been going down the wrong path in that regard. No one likes being yelled at. It's not much fun yelling, either. It's unsettling to both the yeller and the yellee. I believe I contributed to making her sick (asthma can be brought on by nerves, and I don't even know if she has asthma). It was wakeup time for me. Time to be kinder both to her (stop yelling) and to myself (stop worrying). My fears led directly to my anger. It's a fairly common path from fear to anger, and it's always toxic. Consider that anger actually comes from fear, and that it is not a statement of power (as it seems), but a *request* for power. Animals (and people) get all puffed up when they're afraid, and they put on a big, blowsy show to distract us from that fact and convince us that they are instead a force to be reckoned with. Consider armed forces from that perspective. A bunch of international scaredy cats all trying to prove that they're the toughest. When we're fearful, we feel vulnerable. When we're angry, we "feel" empowered, but it's often not genuine. It's usually a lot of bluster leading to high-blood pressure and messy outcomes.

Ultimately, my vet said it sounded like a feline herpes thing and to try adding a little L-Lysine to her diet. I bought L-Lysine powder at the pet health food store and she was right as rain.

On a day that started with fear, I managed to keep calm, cool, collected and challenged myself to be increasingly loving, patient, and kind to me and my cat as I took action to rectify the situation. My job now is to keep both of us calm. She is simply a mirror for me. A mirror that needed dusting.

Living in this topsy-turvy world, my connection to peace comes and goes. I know that it's always available to me, like sap in a tree. The question is how do I tap into it? When I lose my center, how then do I find it again? I use tools. When I woke up feeling uneasy, I immediately made lists of things that would make me feel better, because worry never solves anything. I thought of mellow

people I could talk to, people who inspire me, music that lifts my spirits. I was immediately relieved, knowing I could create comfort for myself. I know that *feeling good* is the key to manifesting what I want.
We want things because we believe they will make us happy. However, if we bypass the "getting stuff" part and just go directly to feeling good, we're ninety percent there to manifesting the things we want. Very often, other things that you didn't know you wanted, but are even better, manifest for you instead. It's good to allow space for the Universe to finesse the specifics of your order. But the feeling tone of happiness, peace and joy are *key* to creating what you want. If you want to be loved, *feel* loved. If you want to be rich, *feel* rich. It's an acting exercise. The more you do it, the better you get.

You're the generator. Not the outside world. It doesn't have what you want. You have what you want, and you activate it with your thoughts and feelings. That's the law of attraction. That's the magic. The outside world *reflects* your interior world. We are constantly in the process of attracting what we're focused on, for good or for bad, and our wants are ever changing. Get in alignment with the vibration of what you want, how you would *feel* if you had it, and then attract away.

This is a period of great spiritual upheaval on Planet Earth. Political revolution. Personal evolution. This big change requires that all old, outdated modes of being be reviewed and discarded. Life is offering us all sorts of tests (irritating strangers) and challenges (sick pets) to really look at who we are, where we are going, and how we choose to react to situations.

Worldwide manipulation, deception and corruption is being revealed left, right and center. I just watched a Frontline piece on the 2010 Michelle O'Connell murder in St. Augustine, Florida. It's still officially a "suicide" but, if you have half a brain, it's obvious that it was domestic violence and murder. But since the perpetrator (her boyfriend) was a sheriff's deputy, the sheriff's department concurred with the murderer's assessment that his girlfriend shot herself right in front of him with his holstered gun, which he then laughed off. Literally. In a taped interview, the perp laughs with his colleague about drinking Bud Lights the night of the murder. "Big ones!" The sheriff's office corruption ran deep and wide but, after public outcry, the case is being reviewed again, years later. I just checked online to find that a second, recent, autopsy has provided powerful evidence that her death was a homicide. The dark *is* being vanquished. Have faith in that, and be a part of that change. Take action and speak up where appropriate.

Speaking of darkness, someone stalked me yesterday. I'm hyper sensitive to my surroundings, and was immediately aware that someone did an abrupt about face behind me as I turned the corner (he was talking loudly to himself). I continued to the next corner and moved out of his way so he could go ahead of me, but he waited to see where I went. I stopped short. He stopped short. I pulled back. So did he. I crossed the street. He did likewise. I turned back to look at him, and he boldly returned my stare. Something was not right. This was in broad daylight and, while I know I am safe, protected, and blessed, I pray to ensure that continued protection, for intentionality is very important. So, call in help when you need it. But having a crazy person breathing down my back, one who was not shy about tailing me, had me rattled.

I spotted a police car parked across the street. Even better, there were two cops standing by it (it could have been parked and empty). I marched directly toward them, convinced I would lose him now, but he boldly walked with me then continued on only a few feet ahead to hide in front of a van. The cops were laughing and enjoying this sunny Fourth of July. I waited respectfully for a few seconds. When one saw I wanted to talk, I said, "I'm sorry to interrupt, but that guy is sorta following me."

"What guy?"

I pointed him out to her. "He's lurking in front of that van."

She walked into the road to eye him then came back. "Where do you live?"

I pointed again. "Down there."

"You get going, and I'll watch him."

I thanked her then went on my way, still nervous about being stalked by someone in such a jaunty mood. He was probably on drugs.

As I walked down my street, a large crowd of men, women, and kids came at me. I could get lost in this crowd. Even with the cop supervising, I took responsibility for my own safety and well-being. I took the opportunity to detour and duck into a heavily landscaped area of a large apartment building and sit on a ledge with my dog. I didn't want crazy guy seeing where I was going, or where I lived. I peeked and saw he was still on the street corner near the cops, loitering, not crossing. I waited a minute longer. Even with a cop watching him, this guy was not going away. I sat for a minute with my dog then walked into a curved driveway instead of staying on the sidewalk, where he could see me. I exited the driveway halfway down the block, that much closer to my home, and caught up with a nice, strong man. I walked just close enough to him to enjoy his unwitting escort.

I was shaken, having never been confronted so directly by a stalker. But I got home safe and sound, albeit with many assists. To me, the real story was that when I needed it, I had at my disposal: daylight, two cops, a crowd to get lost in, a curved driveway that offered a detour, and a de facto bodyguard (not that he knew it). I was totally blessed and protected and I reveled in that. That's what being on your toes and in alignment with your self is all about.

Now, contrast that experience with this one:

I walked by two little girls on the corner. It was hot as heck outside, and they were standing on the street holding a basket of folded papers. I figured they were working for a parent, but turns out they were working for themselves.

They offered me a piece of paper. "Can we give you a compliment?"

"Only if I can give you one first. You're both adorable." I read my custom compliment, "BE HAPPY."

Not exactly a compliment, more of a command, but I liked it just fine. The back of the paper read: "Give someone else a compliment today and spread kindness." They had drawn a smiley face and a heart.

"What moved you to do this?"

"We just want to spread kindness. It was on our bucket list."

"Bucket list? How old are you girls?"

"Twelve."

"Thirteen," they said at the same time.

"Well, you are proof that this world *is* getting better and better and better. Thank you."

They made my day.

Are you offering compliments or nitpicking with people? Are you happy, or irritable? Do you know how to be at peace with yourself?

Do yourself a favor and consciously carve new choices to create a more tranquil life.

CHAPTER 9

Avocado Dude

I had a nightmare about my ex-husband a few days ago. While seemingly innocuous on the surface (not to mention weird), I woke up deeply unsettled. An old, cat claw snaggled towel was pinned to the wall near the bathroom my ex used when he lived with me. There was peanut butter smeared here and there on the cloth. Within the dream, I knew immediately what it meant. He'd had sex with someone, and they'd fooled around, using peanut butter during their encounter. The cat-tattered towel represented his "catting around." But why the peanut butter? Beat the hell out of me.

I confronted him immediately in the dream. "You had sex with her." (She was right there, smirking.) He denied everything, as he always did. Never fessed to a thing. But there were things.

"The towel was hanging in the wind, hung out to dry, left hanging. A throwaway, disposable," a friend suggested.

I found this description of "hung out to dry" online: *To abandon someone who is in need, especially one dependent.* Yes, my ex left me hanging out to dry during our relationship. But was this a throwaway issue? In fact, my ex went on to throw out the kitchen trash in the dream. Not just the trash, but the can itself. I wasn't sure what that meant either. And the peanut butter plain old baffled me.

Wordsmith that I am, the peanut butter explanation came to me a few nights later. The phrase "laying it on thick" popped into my head. It resonated and seemed to explain it all. My ex was always "laying it on thick," whether wheedling for something or waffling out of something, including telling the truth. Peanut butter was an apt metaphor for this behavior and my dream's witty symbol amused me.

The dream's meaning became even clearer days later when I received a call from someone I'd met a few weeks ago. On the last night of a trip to study past life regression upstate, I walked past a fellow I thought I knew, so I said hi. Tall, he seemed to be holding up the roof on the gift shop's porch. He was stretching, or hanging from the eave, or something. I thought it was a guy who worked in the gift shop, someone I'm friendly with. On closer inspection (it was late), I discerned it was not the person that I thought it was, but he and I proceeded to engage in a friendly and somewhat flirty chat.

In talking about my past life regression class, I shared with him my conclusion that I am a true creature of comfort in this lifetime not because I'm a sissy, but because I've suffered enough trauma and deprivation in other lifetimes. Apparently, I've been a soldier several times.

My pain in this lifetime has been emotional. I eschew physical discomfort at all times. He claimed to be the opposite and said he didn't need comfort at all. He said he used to work on Wall Street but that he'd sold his home and was living as a free spirit, going where the wind blew—a Jack Kerouac kinda thing. He traveled and slept in his car.

Dazzling eyes and flirting aside, I became bored so I bid him adieu and retreated to the comfort of my cushy, air-conditioned dorm room with soft sheets. I gave him my card in case he wandered through New York. It occurred to me as I walked through the woods to my room that, in the past, I might have been tempted to hook up with him (though not in these dorms where the walls are paper thin) or at least linger with him longer. But he'd mentioned in passing a desire to be on stage, and that's a huge turnoff for me. I've dated performers, and it never ended well. A wanna-be performer is even worse. So it was a no brainer to say goodnight. I didn't need validation or that kind of "experience" anymore. I feel good about myself, and want to be with a man because he's right for me, not because he's "right there." I took note of my growth and smiled. After years of longing, yearning, and feeling incomplete, I am content now. I am happy.

Never did hear from the guy, which was all well and good with me. I've been very busy since returning from the woods and the Higher Realms (I was in an altered state during much of the five-day past life regression intensive) and it was a difficult adjustment to get back to the harsher vibrations of New York City. It took me a good five days to recover from my crash landing at Port Authority bus terminal. Once restored, I led a psychic development and healing circle workshop (which included a group past life regression) at Namaste Healing Center in Union Square, and the event was a real high. All was well.

I was out doing errands on a sunny Sunday afternoon to further feather my nest and upgrade my bed and bath when he called. Kerouac was in town. "My guidance told me to call you."

I didn't know how to respond to that. "Uh huh."

Don't most men simply act on their desire to get together with a woman? Is "guidance" truly required? Come on. He threw around other new age catch phrases on the phone, perhaps to butter me up since we met at a spiritually oriented joint, but unbeknownst to him, it turned me off. I'm "out there" spiritually but I'm "down here" physically, a fairly feisty New Yorker. My airy-fairy stuff is balanced with plenty of logic, humor and cursing.

"Manifesting...yoga...avocados..." he jabbered on. Avocados? "I was sitting on Thirty-Fourth Street and Fifth Avenue, got up, and when I went to sit back down, there was an avocado. What do you think it means?"

Listen, I had enough trouble with my peanut butter, now I have to figure out his avocado? "I have no idea."

Rogue, rolling avocados mean nothing to me, on Thirty-Fourth Street or anywhere else. He was sure it was a sign. Well, he'd just have to do the same due diligence with his subconscious that I had with mine, or Google the green fruit like I did. Seems avocados represent a bunch of things, including lust.

He asked if I wanted to meet that afternoon for coffee. I hadn't been on a date in ages, I had time, and I was dressed nicely. I agreed. We met at an upscale health-food-y place with outdoor seating an hour later. I was wearing Upper East Side garb, as I was fully owning who I am—someone who has, someone who wants, someone who enjoys. I'm not abstemious in my tastes or behaviors. I'm a sensual spiritualist.

He was there in all his glory. Baseball cap, flip-flops, shorts, gray ponytail. He was channeling The Dude from *The Big Lebowski*. It was all becoming clear to me, all the more so in the light of day on the sidewalk, not under the stars in the woods. This guy definitely tied in with my ex-husband, sparkling eyes and all. They were both big kids. My dream had been a premonition.

By now it was two p.m., and I'd not had lunch. I told him I was hungry and asked if he was going to eat. He wasn't. He ordered a hibiscus tea. Cognizant that he might pay for this date, since he'd asked me out, I abstained (against my religion) from food and ordered a cup of hot tea with cream to abate my hunger. I wasn't going to put him out.

I don't remember what we (he) talked about because it just bored me to pieces. His yoga practice. His breathing. I dunno. In short order, I was dying to get out of there. Another narcissist, wanna-be performer/writer/dreamer. Oh, and he didn't actually work in finance (as the statement "I worked on Wall Street" would imply). He worked in "communications." I finally discerned the actual meaning of that clarification. He was the phone guy. Do you think the guy who sells hot dogs on the corner of Wall and Front Streets tells potential dates that he works on Wall Street, too?

Avocado Dude was "laying it on thick," as my ex had when he told me he was an "account executive" for the cable company when I met him. In reality, he knocked on doors in The Bronx to sign people up for HBO and Cinemax. What my ex tried at twenty-eight is not so cute when attempted at fifty-five. Actually, it's not cute at any age. Just speak the truth. I might actually like you. But at least you'll enable me to see you for who you are, not who you wish you were.

Avocado Dude observed, "Blah, blah, blah…I think it's what you and I have in common."

I don't remember what it was, because I had no idea what he was rambling on about, nor did I see anything similar between us at all. I like beds. He like cars. I wash my hair. He wears baseball caps.

Avocado Dude mentioned a girl he'd just visited for a week to "tie up some unfinished business" (read between the lines: sex). He'd also visited someone else after he met me. Another woman? In fact, the cell phone he called me from had a woman's name on the caller ID. Who the heck was she? Did he just drive from woman to woman? More damn peanut butter.

He presented me with the avocado in question, wrapped in a paper bag he said he'd also found on the street. Was this supposed to impress me? The avocado had a cut on it. He offered it for me to hold, but made sure I knew it was not for me to keep. Was I supposed to read it like a crystal ball?

"Yup. Definitely an avocado." I handed it back to him.

I made a hasty exit after just over an hour, something that seemed to take him by surprise. As I got up, I asked, "Would you like money for the tea?"

He hesitated only a second before caving. "Sure."

I gave him $5.

I was incensed when I left. I was pissed at him for being boring and cheap and a liar and just pissed that this had happened to me again. That this "type" had happened to me again.

And yet, what had really happened? Not only did I not marry this dazzler, I didn't even sleep with him. So, I had a cup of tea. I had dabbled with "The Dude." This was dating nightmare "lite." I'd never even had an inkling of an urge for "more" with this loser. This is how your soul knows you've really done the work and learned the lesson. When you're confronted with the same crap at a different time, how do you respond? I had passed the test. Even better, my nightmare (intuition) had warned me about what was coming, and I loved that.

I dated a very wealthy fellow years ago who fancied

himself a "man of nature." He spent little cash, especially on me, and perhaps thought it meaningful when, during an open-top ride in the countryside in his sports car, he handed me an acorn top. It was a "gift."

"They told me to give this to you" he said, without explaining who "they" were.

I didn't bother to ask. Clearly, they were the "voices" in his cheap-ass head. I tossed it over the side of the car. "Tell them I already have one."

This same guy gave me a rock once. It wasn't even *his* rock. It was *my* rock. I found it on the ground and showed it to him because it was heart shaped. He took it from me, despite my protestations, then returned it to me weeks later painted red. Some fucking present. He said nothing when he handed *my* rock back to me. He probably thought it was "from the heart." Actually, it was "from the ground." There comes a time to just open up your freaking wallet.

Then there was the artist I had a fling with. It sizzled initially but fizzled quickly. After sleeping with me on two "dates," he accepted my offer of $5 to split our single Chinese entree (this was dinner). I didn't expect him to accept, but lo and behold, he did. I had been sympathetic to his starving artist status at the time, a sympathy I no longer extend.

The Dude's guidance had been right on for him to call me. I was meant to confront this type of loser again. I could not ignore the irritation, nor "breathe" it away. I'd have to bitch it out. It was too close to home (Ex-husband! Selfish artists!) to let go without reacting. The event held a *huge* emotional charge for me. Which is why I had the nightmare a few days prior. It was a heads-up.

In fact, my friend Nicole had given me a message not long before that I didn't like too well. I'd just experienced something minor but annoying, and she said I'd have more of the same challenges or tests coming up. Well, I don't know about you, but having survived several thousand challenges, tests, and irritations in this lifetime already, I was not eager to have more. However, she added that I'd be able to shake them off, to laugh them off easily now, an indication of my progress. Having just survived yet one more test, seeing how relatively innocuous yet *hugely* symbolic it was for me, I got the point. I was not hurt. I was out an hour of my time and five dollars (believe me, my ex got away with far more). I don't feel sorry for people anymore, and especially not men I might date. I'm no longer in the broken-wing-mending business. It's because I don't feel sorry for myself anymore. I used to extend to others the sympathy and compassion that I myself craved.

I cut The Dude loose to hang in the breeze.

It doesn't make me more spiritual to get involved with users, losers, liars, and cheaters. That's not compassion. That's stupidity and hanging out with the wrong crowd. My anger also does not make me less spiritual. It is simply an indication that something is *wrong* and needs correcting. In this case, it was an Avocado Alert.

What did "manifesting" an avocado on Thirty-Fourth Street mean? Avocados can symbolize self-love, self-worth, transforming inner beauty into external beauty, balancing male and female energies, balance between opposites, lust, and love. Avocados are also associated with cojones, which they look like, and which Avocado Dude obviously had. But I just think it meant he was about to lay a big, green egg. Which he did. With me.

Back to my nightmare. In the end, the trash was thrown out, all of it, even the can. I can release the past now, throw it all away, especially the pain and discomfort. I can make new choices.

This story has a happy ending. I found five bucks on

the street yesterday, and I was ecstatic, for it was a symbol. The Universe reimbursed the money I was out from the lousy date. No, I didn't get my hour back, but that's okay. I have this story. The return of my fiver was sweet confirmation that this lesson is complete. My money was refunded, as surely as the trash was taken out in my dream. Out with the bad. In with the good,

Avocado Dude wasn't a free spirit. He was homeless. He can sleep in his car and lay as many avocados as he likes, while I enjoy pillows and peace in my private paradise.

CHAPTER 10

The Mystical Bike Shop (An Interlude)

A bicycle doesn't typically come to mind when seeking respite from the sun, but that's what this guy was hiding behind on a hot, Saturday morning in New York City. A pasty fellow who looked to be forty was ahead of me in line during Summer Streets (Park Avenue shuts down for half a day, three weekends a summer).

"This is what sucks about New York," he griped.

"What?"

We were in line to receive free bicycle helmets, what could be so bad?

"Long lines" he groused, as if it was obvious.

"That's what makes the city great," I responded.

He was incredulous. "Long lines?"

"No, lots of people. They go hand in hand. Not to mention, we get free helmets."

"Well, long lines suck," pale guy restated.

I was unamused by his sour attitude. "You're getting free stuff in a big city, what do you expect?"

The guy crouched behind his CitiBike (rented from the city's bike sharing program) seeking shelter from the shadow cast by its seat and frame. The guy was thin, but not skeletal. How could the bike's shadow possibly help? The line was long, and progress was slow. They were fitting everyone for proper helmet size and handing out colorful brain-shaped erasers (wear that helmet!) to the kids. I saw Crouching Tiger smile and took this as an opening.

"Are you hiding from the sun?" I teased.

He was paler than me, which is pretty hard to accomplish. The guy needed a little sunshine. Turns out he wasn't smiling, he was smirking. His whining recommenced. "They should have tents out here to protect us! It's hot!"

Unbelievable. "Is this your wedding?" I shot back. "What do you want, champagne and caviar, too?"

"Well, the workers have a tent!" he retorted.

There were twenty workers. There were hundreds of us. "That's because they're here *all day*. You're here half an hour. You're getting a free helmet. This is not your opening night."

When all was said and done, we both got shiny new helmets. Mine's a silver/white number. It's nice, but he got the color I coveted, lime green. What did he do as he exited the arena, free helmet on head? Stuck out his tongue like a three year-old. I guess he didn't like the color. But really, he didn't like anything, did he? Not the sun, not the heat, not the lines, not his helmet.

There were tons of people happily milling around. I saw an Indian family who had waited patiently in line ahead of grumpy guy and me. Everyone—father, mother, two kids, and grandma (in a sari)—had a helmet on their head as they departed the area and strolled down Park Avenue. Not one of them had a bike.

People bike up and down Park Avenue during Summer Streets. Some walk or run. It's a combination party and parade. There are various booths with promotional events, musical performances, and exercise and dance classes on the sidewalk. The bike route passed right by the downtown store where I bought my bike, and it reminded me to get a free tune-up.

My dog was with me in the bike basket, and I reveled in all the sights this celebratory day offered. A waterslide by City Hall and the courts considerably lightened the area's weighty governmental tone. There was free (sponsored) coconut water, mobile tap water fountains set up by the city just for this day, hammocks, sand, music, and dancing. Everything was flowing. A little girl (clearly the next Beyoncé) was dancing so well and boisterously at a year and a half that she had a paparazzi like horde of humans (myself included) videotaping her moves.

My bike store participated in the day's festivities by selling biking shoes and helmets on the sidewalk for cheap. They were in snazzy, Valerie-friendly colors. But they were too big, both the shoes and the helmets. Since I'm very good at attracting what I want, I went online later, determined to find the snazzy shoes for a good price. They were not on special anywhere. Oh well. I really had missed a great deal.

The store was too crowded to get my complimentary tune-up during Summer Streets Saturday, so I returned to the store the next day, curious to see if I could work some shoe magic, too. Their website indicated that the store had one pair in my size, so while my bike was being worked on, I jokingly asked if they had any helmets for my puppy (who was securely bungee-corded into my bike basket), and if they had any more of those fun biking shoes.

One of the guys remembered me and my dog from the day before. He sent me next door to their auxiliary shop, and said if they had them, to refer the salesperson back to him. He would give me the great deal from yesterday. The prospect of success was in the air.

They had them in two vibrant shades. Another lovely guy assisted me, told me which color he liked better (it helped sway my decision) and said he'd give me the fabulous price break. So, the elusive offer came from two angels.

I'm not sure how it got started, but I began talking about mysticism (not terribly unusual for me). I told him about the recent past life regression intensive I took, and the upcoming psychic development class I was about to teach. He seemed startled then shyly confessed that he was quite psychic himself. He called over a young female associate, an astrologer, and the three of us had a brief psychic pow-wow. He said that the girl, the guy tuning up my bike, and he were all in their last karmic round of incarnations.

I can't say I agree with that kind of assessment. It's not something you can verify, and it's out of your hands anyway. It's sort of like deciding you're going to graduate before your school confirms your eligibility. But I liked him and the gang anyway, living out their last lives or not.

"Merlin," "Kate," and "Mercurio" were all magicians. They loved their jobs. They were happy people. And I had Technicolor biking shoes to supercharge my ride home.

Do you seek miracles, and thereby create them? Or do you grumble about free helmets and look for cover behind bicycles? One path opens doors wide, while the other seals them firmly shut.

CHAPTER 11

Heaven's Gate

I was off on a grand adventure. For someone who rarely travels, I had two trips booked practically back to back. One to upstate New York to study past-life regression with Dr. Brian Weiss. The other, to study in Toronto with renowned energy healer Adam McLeod, a young man who has been healing folks of serious illness since he was a minor. He's now a microbiologist MD with a naturopathic cancer clinic in western Canada. Both were last-chance study opportunities for me. After many years of touring, Adam was discontinuing workshops to focus on his private practice. Brian was slowing down his teaching schedule because…well, he's old. I'd had both of them on my radar for years, but it was now or never if I was going to study with either of them.

I hadn't flown in ages, and I hadn't been to Toronto in fourteen years. I'd be away less than forty-eight hours, in which I was to meet with a book reviewer right after landing Friday, attend an all-day workshop Saturday, and spend time with two other friends, one of whom I'd just met at the past-life regression intensive. It was an action packed two days.

I was traveling light with (basically) two pairs of underwear and a toothbrush. Instead of lugging my heavy, cumbersome passport I took my nifty US Passport Card for which I'd paid a premium when renewing my passport. I considered taking my passport as backup, but decided against it as I wanted to get my money's worth from this lovely, wafer-thin option. That's what I bought it for. I travel rarely so I'm lucky I remembered it at all, but I knew this card was good for travel to Canada and Mexico only and I was eager to use it. It was passport "lite."

I decided to try public transportation to LaGuardia on this hot August morning. It could be done easily from my home, and all for $2.75. My flight was at eight forty-five a.m. I was up by five, and at the airport by seven. Perfect. After waiting fruitlessly on the wrong check-in line, I was sent to check-in via machine, most of which were broken. By the time I got a spot, the machine rejected my passport card. I'd had it with lines, so I rushed to the front counter.

"Excuse me, the machine is not accepting my passport."

The young ticket agent looked at my US Passport Card. "That's not a passport. You need a passport."

I started stuttering, the disastrous implications immediately hitting me like a two by four to the head. "What do you mean it's not a passport? It says 'US Passport Card.'"

"That card is for land and sea travel only. Boats and cars."

"You're kidding me. I have to be on that flight. What do I do?"

"Go home and get your passport."

"But I don't have time! I'll never make my flight!"

"You have to go get your passport."

"Please. Please. I have to be on this flight. I have a business meeting at noon!" I showed my card to the other, older agent in the hope that he might wave me through. Uncomfortable, he glanced away from me then back down at his monitor. Desperation and begging were getting me nowhere. I had my driver's license, Canadian "boating pass," and credit cards. Couldn't they tell it was me? What they were asking for was impossible.

With the clock ticking, I kicked into overdrive and did the only thing I could—try to make it happen. I dashed over to a cab and blurted "You have to get me home and back as fast as possible. I need to get my passport!"

I told him how to go, but he claimed there was traffic getting onto the Fifty-Ninth Street Bridge. "See?" He pointed at a slow lane. He suggested the RFK Bridge. Where the hell was that? They keep renaming everything. I was in no position to argue and took his advice. We drove *way* the hell north (yes, totally out of the way) to take the Triboro (now RFK) Bridge (with an additional toll) which then led us directly into hideous Friday morning traffic heading south on the FDR Drive. Some "save."

Profoundly stressed, I squeezed my wallet so hard that, if it were possible to juice, concentrate of wallet would have been extracted. Instead, *I* produced the moisture, streaming steam heat like a humidifier.

I intermittently blurted *"JESUS!"* like someone with Christian Tourrettes. The driver's name was Sheikh and he'd just have to cope with my choice of deity. If I knew how to pray to Allah, I would have. Right now, I just focused on massaging my wallet with an intensity that should have macerated its contents, especially my lousy "US Passport Card."

My breath was shallow and sporadic so I strained to catch some oxygen. The thought of missing this once in a lifetime weekend was unfathomable to me. I had planned everything so meticulously, how did this happen? *How?* I had misunderstood the purpose of the US Passport Card, that's how. It's for people with canoes, rollerblades, kayaks, and skateboards. As we got closer to my home. I took control of our route. "Get off at Sixty-Third Street! Leave me on First Avenue! I'll run home while you drive around the block!"

He had to follow traffic, I didn't. I gave him my address. Save for my wallet and keys, I left the bags in the cab. I didn't have time to take them with me or the luxury of worrying about their safety. This *had* to work. I raced diagonally across First Avenue toward oncoming traffic, which was starting to pick up. I thrust my hand out like a traffic cop to facilitate my own crossing. I didn't worry about rules and regulations from here on out. I had one objective. To get on that plane. I shot upstairs, bolted into my bedroom with a ferocity that scared the bejesus out of my two cats, and ripped my passport out of its folder in the bowels of my desk. As I came downstairs, Sheikh was gently pulling in front of my building. Like buttah. I slid into the cab.

I continued to take the reins for this ride. I told Sheikh to take the Fifty-Ninth Street Bridge back this time, rush hour traffic be damned. There was no escaping it anywhere. I called my friend Bill who lives in Queens, and he telephonically held my hand. He was my airport "labor and delivery coach" while I breathed between contractions. Bill gave me running commentary on how we were doing route-wise.

Apparently, according to Bill, my driver could have done better. He could have taken Northern Boulevard in Queens, which functions like a parkway, instead of the crappy road under the elevated train that he took, which hit light after light after light after light (after light). It's distinctly possible that he had taken me down two garden paths in an effort to make more money instead of helping me to achieve my objective. If he did, that's on his soul. That being said, he was a safe driver. I got back to LaGuardia with thirty minutes until takeoff. I thanked Sheikh from the bottom of my heart and gave him a big tip. He had done what I'd asked him to. The cab cost $80. So much for my $2.75 subway and bus ride earlier in the day.

I raced to the front of the line like a madwoman. There was hardly anyone there. The two agents who'd seen me frantic before were still there. "I made it! I did it!" I gasped. "Here's my passport!" I flashed it in the air, exultant, breathless, relieved, and *so* proud of my accomplishment.

This was *The Amazing Race* and *The Wizard of Oz* combined. I, Dorothy, had vanquished the Wicked Witch of the West and had produced her broom as demanded by the Wizard.

I noticed the young man helping me had an "in training" badge on. This did not bode well. He was clearly waiting for the older man to assist him. Since the older man was assisting someone who seemed not at all to be in a rush, I butt in, "Excuse me, I'm about to miss my flight. Will you please help me?" The two officials looked at the screen and started typing. I talked with the girl next to me, a tall drink of water with long reddish hair and a guitar, whose transaction I had interrupted. I apologized. She didn't mind.

"Singer songwriter?" I intuited.

"Yup." She smiled warmly. She was totally relaxed.

I was convinced I'd get on my flight. They weren't so sure, and I couldn't understand why. I had done everything they asked me to. I had left my perfectly good place in line with my perfectly official looking but useless US Passport Card to run home in morning rush hour traffic, and against all odds, get back in record time with the document they requested.

The two men looked up from the screen, "You might have to take the next flight."

My stomach seized. "What? But I got here in time! It's thirty minutes away! Can't you call and tell them I'm *here*, that I'm coming *now*? I *have* to be on that flight! I have a business meeting at noon!"

They stared at the screen again and typed some more. They were reading and writing with the urgency of someone posting on Facebook. I couldn't understand why they didn't just give me my boarding pass.

"*Please* tell them I'm here! Please?"

A pause, then the younger man spoke. "Can you run?"

"Yes!!! YES!!! I'm a *totally* fast runner! Tell them I'm running now!"

They handed me a boarding pass.

I grabbed it and yelled as I ran, "Thank you so much!!!"

The race was now on to reach Gate A-7. I ran like the wind until I hit travel security. I'd completely forgotten all about that. I frantically pushed through the long lines. "Excuse me! Excuse me!" When I rushed the front I gasped in explanation to the hordes I was bypassing, "I'm about to miss my flight!" My panic was clear.

The singer songwriter was somehow ahead of me at the front of the security line. How was that humanly possible? Mystic that I am, I now wonder if she was human at all, or an angel there to bring some peace to me on a frantic day. "Go ahead of me."

She smiled warmly, again. I took my shoes off per "security rules" (what the hell is that all about?) walked through the metal detector straight into that horrible cat-scan machine, the one I swore never to go into (being against radiation of all kinds). There went my promise. They radiated me.

By the time I realized where I was, the round glass doors had sealed around me. The sign directed me to put my arms over my head, like I was under arrest. All part of the desired effect in our new Police State, post 9/11. Create fear and establish control by treating *all* of us like suspects, guilty until proven innocent, under constant, perpetual, inescapable and totally *un-American* surveillance. I exited the MRI monster (which probably took a year off of my life) and grabbed my computer as it rolled out of its own X-ray exam, but the singer gently touched my hand and stopped me.

"That's my computer."

Oh my God, it was her Apple, not mine. Mortified, I apologized, then saw mine coming down the conveyer rollers. There was no time to put my high-heel, buckle-up sandals back on. I grabbed my sandals, computer, shoulder bag, and carry on luggage and prepared to sprint again.

"Wait!" The guard stopped me. "What's in this bottle?" They were holding my water bottle, a very pricey stainless steel number.

"Water!"

"You'll have to go outside to dump the water."

"Outside where?"

"All the way outside."

God knows I was thirsty from all the sweating I had done. "Keep it!" I started running again.

I thought my "Canadian Driver's License and Dog Paddling Pass" was a passport. You think I knew about the water restriction? What the hell can a terrorist do with water? Douse the pilot? Moisten a flight attendant? It could melt the Wicked Witch of the West, that's what it could do. And it could hydrate me.

Our security rules are insane. They are meant to chasten us into submission, *not* to stop the bad guys. Why does no one complain about this nonsense? We're not safer. We are being fucked with. The inmates are running the asylum. It's Orwell's *1984* in living color. Orwell's book was intended as a warning, not an instruction manual.

With laser beam focus, I dashed barefoot past gate after gate. Now I was starring in *Run, Lola, Run*. I raced like the wind through the maze of LaGuardia security and the terminal itself, clocking in at under ten minutes (is there an Olympic "Airport" category?) Panting, I reached gate A-7 (it was, of course, the *very* last gate) and, panting, handed the Gate Queen my boarding pass. The Bionic Woman could have done no better.

"Here!" I said breathlessly.

She looked at the paper and, with a blank face, said "This is for the next flight. Go sit over there."

"What? But I'm on *this* flight! They told me I could get on *this* flight!"

"Look at your boarding pass."

I glanced down. It had a new flight number on it. "But—but—but—(total stuttering)—I have to be on *this* flight! I have a business meeting at noon!"

"You were *late*. You lost your seat," she snapped. She glanced at me with cold eyes before returning civilly to her well-behaved customers. A tough, no-nonsense New York matron (or was it dominatrix?) she was in no mood. She had a plane to board and I was in the way. I stuttered some more, my adrenaline, breath and blood still pumping full force, though my body had stopped moving.

"This flight was overbooked and there are people

flying standby. You're on the next flight. Sit over there." She meant, "Sit over there, *stupid*."

She probably thought I was some late, irresponsible person. She would not be interested to hear my explanation that I'm always on time, never miss a trick, and never lose a thing. I just made a terrible mistake that day. Still on metabolic fire, I knew enough not to antagonize her. She had the charm and ease of a prison warden.

The guys at check-in up front knew what was up when they handed me a boarding pass for the next flight, while leading me to believe that I could run and catch mine. Did they think I was an idiot, too? I was desperate, in shock, but not demanding. I was, however, persistent. I was too wired to sit down. I moved away (so as not to crowd her) but remained well within Gate Queen's sightline. She would not forget about me as I waited patiently (but fervently) to get on that flight.

I stared longingly at the big plane I should have been on. It sat there, taunting me. Other people continued to get on. A firm believer in miracles, I hoped and prayed that they could squeeze me on somehow. I mean, I'm not even that big.

I spotted the customer service counter nearby and thought "They can help me!" I wanted to discuss whether it was standard operating procedure to give someone's ticket away with thirty whole, juicy American minutes to go until flight time. Really, I was hoping they'd say, "That's outrageous! You poor girl, after all you went through. We're putting you right on that plane! You can sit with the pilot."

They asked to see my boarding pass then leaned in to examine it. The one holding it promptly tore it in half. I was incredulous. "Why did you do that? That was my boarding pass!"

"That's not your boarding pass. That's someone

else's boarding pass. They never should have given it to you. The second flight is overbooked with people flying standby. You probably won't get on that flight, either."

These corrections officers liked me about as much as the warden. My eyes practically popped out of my head. They didn't care about me one little bit, these hardened New York women. They treated me like a felon requesting parole. So much for customer "service."

The bottom line was I simply wasn't a priority. It was a huge economy flight overbooked with standby. I was traveling with miles, and not even from Air Canada, so I was chump change. My only hope for the ten-thirty a.m. flight was now gone too, with their little paper shredding stunt. I now had no paperwork to confirm *any* reservation, including my return flight. The men at the front desk had kept my printout for everything. The gate door closed. My eight forty-five flight took off.

I was now hoping against hope to get on the ten-thirty flight. I could still make my lunch appointment. I texted my lunch partner, a woman who has reviewed my three books, with the latest travel info. There didn't seem to be many passengers for this second flight. Maybe I had a chance. Another guy who'd been loitering said he was flying standby. They gave *him* a boarding pass. Perhaps there was hope, but even still, how did he get ahead of me? I glared at him.

I had been stuttering all morning and now had the potential to develop a serious facial tic, on the order of Chief Inspector Dreyfus's in *The Pink Panther*. Instead, I went to the ladies room every ten minutes and peed profusely each time. I must have lost five pounds just urinating.

As I entered the ladies room again, an older woman recognized me from my last pee. "You see?" (I didn't see anything.) "And it only gets worse with age."

To add to my travails I was receiving urinary threats from a senior.

I sat down then restlessly wandered back to the Gate Queen. "Customer service just tore up my boarding pass for the second flight. How am I ever going to get to Toronto?"

"You'll just have to wait flight by flight to see which one you can get on."

"But this could go on all day!" I shook my head in disbelief. I was in a state of shock.

The cortisol continued to pump. I was still in serious fight or flight mode. Gate Queen clearly didn't give a shit about my plight, so I faded away again. I continued to run back and forth to the ladies room. I guess my body was trying to lighten its load in case I had to run for my life again. I cased every potential flight like a hungry predator, and every passenger as a competitor. They were taking my seat. My action packed weekend was slipping away, second by second.

I forced myself to breathe slower and to take in more air. I calmed down some, but my cortisol levels were still off the charts. The movie *Argo* came to mind, a movie I loved and wondered how in hell those people kept it together under such extreme, sustained stress. I now know the answer. Because they had to. Because their lives depended on it. I felt that mine did, too. I was going to Toronto for less than forty-eight hours and had three people and one all-day workshop to squeeze into that limited time frame. My return flight was at six-thirty a.m. on Sunday. As each hour whittled away, there went the finely tuned social apparatus I had designed. I didn't have Iranian militants looking for me. However, I did have mean female airline employees holding me back at the gate.

I unobtrusively sniffed the people around me. Did

the guy sitting next to me have terrible body odor? I couldn't tell, so I smelled my shirt. Not me. Must have been him. I kept sniffing and smelling from time to time and eventually came to the terrible conclusion at the end of the day that it *was* me. It wasn't even a human smell. More like skunk.

I had planned meticulously for this trip, including my decision not to bring my redundant, "bulky" passport as backup ID. Now, my life was flashing before my eyes. Interestingly, I'd just read that airports are a locus for psychic fear (and hauntings, along with dental offices, court rooms, and hospitals, which I already knew about). Fear and ghosts go hand in hand. Was the airport's general fear imprint (energy vibration) amplifying my own? I guess lots of people are afraid of flying. Add the intense "terrorist" bureaucracy (three point *five* ounces of shampoo is a security risk, my ass) and you've got a swirling vortex of anxiety.

Gate Queen called me to the desk. She handed me a boarding pass! All was resolved, and relatively quickly in the larger scheme of things. I thanked her effusively. I texted my lunch date to let her know I'd only be half an hour late. (If I'd been on the original flight, I was going to use the extra time to relax, unpack, and swim, but that plan was blown out of the water). Relieved and happy, I let the other two friends I'd called for support know that all was well.

Gate Queen called me back to her desk. "Can I see your boarding pass?"

I handed it to her. She tore it in half. Apparently, they like to hand out boarding passes then tear them up. Something to while away the hours. I was reduced to a state I can imagine is similar to the crushed condition torture victims reach (with no disrespect to their extreme suffering intended).

This was psychological torture. One becomes numb.

I texted everyone again to let them know that I was back in limbo. It seemed I would never get back to Kansas.

There was nothing I could do to force this issue. I had tried in good faith to beg and plead. I was neither obstreperous nor abusive. I was just desperate, plain and simple, and now I was spent. No one was helping. I think the two guys up front initially had tried to help me by giving me a boarding pass of sorts for the second flight, but they also could have told me I'd already lost my first seat and not encouraged me to run for it. It made no sense. I had done everything the Wizard of Oz asked me to do. Against all odds, I raced to Manhattan and got back in one hour. They asked if I could run to the gate, and I ran like a cheetah on amphetamines. The Wizard had led me on and let me down, just like he had Dorothy. I did everything humanly possible, no, *superhumanly* possible to make my flight. All for naught. They were treating me like the village idiot.

They may have thought, indeed, that I *was* an idiot, but I found out from a friend who had recently traveled to Toronto that during her check-in two other women were in the same damn boat I was in at Air Canada's ticket counter. It was *one* boat the US Freaking Passport Card didn't work on. One woman brought a passport card instead of a passport, like I had. The other woman was simply "passport free." At least I knew that Canada was a foreign country. Had the US Passport website made perfectly clear the peripatetic limitations of the US Passport Card when I ordered it online, I'd not have wasted the extra $20 (it's now $30) when renewing my actual passport.

There was now a man working along with Gate Queen at A-7's boarding pass desk. He seemed nicer. He smiled at people, where she did not, and he'd witnessed the shredding of my second boarding pass. Trying to avoid her at all costs, I sidled up to him during a quiet moment and asked what was next. He said they'd keep trying to get me on a flight.

"This could go on all day. Oh my God." I'm very pale but I was whiter than normal just then. All my fluids had drained, from blood to urine. I continued dehydrating by adding tears to the mix.

I sat down and started to cry. Not sobs, just tears of sadness, confusion, frustration, and exhaustion. My body had sustained a state of acute tension for hours. I finally started to release, and it felt good. My high alert status softened into submission. Cognizant that my tears could be useful, I approached the nice man again with a pink nose and one tear prominently dripping from my left cheek. "Is there even a chance I'll get on the ten-thirty flight?"

He softened. "We're doing the best we can."

"Am I guaranteed nothing? Am I even on a list?"

The man showed me that I was at the top of a computer list, but explained that it guaranteed nothing. He directed me to gate A-5 to wait for the eleven-thirty flight. There was nothing else to say. Ten-thirty took off. I slunk away.

Instead of contemplating a day of mass defeat, I determined to take this torment one flight at a time.

I sat down in A-5's smaller waiting area and started to relax into whatever this Twilight Zone was. My adrenaline abated enough that I finally felt hunger pangs. I pulled out my snack and moved toward the windows to eat in peace and relative privacy. I had a hard-boiled egg, half an avocado, and some dried seaweed. An Indian family next to me was eating standard American airport crap, hot dogs. How humans survive on constant processed food is beyond me. Then again, numbers for cancer, diabetes, and obesity (for starters) continue to rise. It's not called SAD (Standard American Diet) for nothing.

I returned to my bag and original seat and found an older gentleman now sitting to my left. He had a full head of white hair and a little white moustache. The young guy to my right was buff, bald, and tattooed.

The older fellow was chatty. "So, ziss is *your* seat."

"Yes, it is."

He had an accent, but I couldn't place it, so I asked. Peter was German. There was no excuse for my missing that one, my father was born in Germany, and I have a good ear for dialects. But I was missing a lot of things that morning. Just add his accent to the pile.

"I don't have a boarding pass," I confessed.

He leaned in and smiled conspiratorially. "Neizer do I. I alvays fly stendby."

"How does that work?" I queried.

He explained that he'd worked thirty years for Air Canada as a ticket agent and he'd been to Barbados thirty-three times. I still don't know how standby works, but I now had an amiable compadre who was in the same boat I was. My stomach full, my bladder empty, things were starting to looking up on all fronts.

Minutes later two names were called. His. And mine. We looked at each other and got up. We approached the bench together. The Gate Queen who had kept me at bay for hours handed us each a boarding pass. I thanked her like someone who'd been granted a stay of execution. Peter and I sat down, clutching our papers.

"I love you!" I exclaimed, overcome with relief. "Are we sitting together?"

"I don't sink so. Interestingly, I am leaving my wife of twenty-four years, so ze position is open."

I had dated a senior citizen, whom this jaunty guy actually reminded me a fair bit of, but one animated senior was enough for my dance card. "Thank you, but I won't be applying for the spot."

He surreptitiously offered me complimentary new earbuds from his pocket as we approached the plane's portal, obviously from a stash amassed from his frequent flying.

For some strange reason, I now had two boarding passes for this flight. I'm not sure how or when that happened. This was an Express plane, and much smaller than the two earlier mega flights I had missed.

There were only two seats per row here, which suited me just fine. I even got a window, which I love. I settled in, snug as a bug in a rug, allowing myself to finally relax.

The main flight attendant walked all the way to the back of the plane, where I was buckled in.

She eyed me. "There you are."

Oh, no, not again. What did she want?

She handed me a piece of paper, which turned out to be yet a third boarding pass, of all things, then smiled warmly. "Enjoy the flight."

I was baffled, but at least they were handing them out now and not tearing them up anymore. Not a one for hours, and now three for the same flight.

The flight was short and sweet, complete with delicious coffee. I was in seventh heaven, though I still kept sniffing the guy next to me for body odor as I hadn't yet figured out that the aroma I discerned was emanating from my own person.

I now had to rush to make my lunch appointment. My next assignment was to find Terminal 1 Port S-5 to get the hotel shuttle bus that ran every twenty-five minutes. Had I arrived on time at ten-thirty a.m. as scheduled, I knew the applicable shuttle departure times, but could not for the life of me do the twenty-five minute math cycle for two and a half hours later. I just had to get to the bus stop and trust in my fate.

I was held up again, waiting for everyone to deplane, since I was all the way in the back. Once out, I bolted out of the gate like a racehorse. It was *Run, Lola, Run* again, with me dashing in front of everyone who strolled, dawdled, and lollygagged with their families. I had to get through customs. More machines. I pulled out my customs paper and tried to scan it, but it wouldn't fit. There was a perforation I hadn't seen, so I tore the excess paper off and slid the form in, like when scanning a voting ballot in New York City. It spat the form out and demanded that I fill in sections three and four. Good grief.

My adrenaline was pumping again. A sweet officer came over to help me. At least the Canadians were nice. The missing sections were for Canadians.

Having already confirmed I was American, I had left the Canadian part blank. Seemed fairly obvious to do so, but no, it was required that I draw three separate lines through the three blank spaces. More bureaucratic nonsense. She handed me a pen. My lines were as jagged as an EKG's.

She ferried me over to the customs guard, a very formidable, big bald guy named Ryan. "Good morning," he said in very relaxed fashion.

I returned his greeting, but a bit faster.

"Business or pleasure?"

"Business. I'm *rushing* to get to a lunch appointment," I said fast as I could.

He slowed down the beats per minute with his reply. "What kind of business?"

"I'm a writer and a teacher"

"What do you write about?"

I pulled out *Raving Violet*, my first book. "Here, but I don't have an extra copy, this is for the reviewer I'm meeting for lunch."

"I couldn't take it anyway. I'd have to fill out a bunch of customs forms and that would take a *long* time. What's it about?"

Dear God. A simple explanation didn't satisfy him, so I went on to explain that I was studying with a renowned Canadian energy healer who's also a microbiologist MD with a naturopathic cancer practice in Vancouver. "I teach healing and psychic development in New York City."

He started scrawling big letters and symbols (which I'm fairly confident indicated that I was nuts) on my form with his red grease pencil. But he let me go and gave me my walking papers.

I started racing again and handed off the official pass with red sigils that indicated I was insane to one last guard. "Where's Terminal One?"

"You're in it," the guard answered.

I scanned the signs for ground transportation. "Where's Port S-Five?"

"Go down a level to your left," someone else answered.

I finally located a down escalator to the left which came to a dead end. No S-5. I ran to the right and passed a pilot who was smoking while waiting for ground transport. "Do you know where S-5 is?"

He smiled and pointed to the right. I smiled and sighed. Pant, pant, run.

When was that shuttle bus? I finally saw Ports S-3 and S-4. Not sixty seconds after I made it to Port S-5, my hotel shuttle bus pulled up. Perfect divine timing. The shuttle was brand new and all mine. Not a soul was inside, except for my lovely driver. As we pulled into my airport hotel (which was literally ten minutes away) he pointed out all the Secret Service men planted in the bushes and behind cars. The Prime Minister of Canada, Stephen Harper, was staying at my hotel. Stalking me, as far as I was concerned. A few weeks ago my local Whole Foods was surrounded by cop cars and flashing lights. I thought someone had opened gunfire, or maybe Beyoncé was hungry. Nope. It was Secretary of State John Kerry recovering from a broken leg and surgery with the help of a cane, grazing at my local salad bar. He picked at the greens while the Secret Service cased the joint, and I bought ingredients for lasagna.

First Kerry, and now Harper. Very suspicious.

My lunch date, book enthusiast and reviewer Eniko Tolnai, a Canadian of Hungarian descent, was waiting for me in the lobby. After hours of drama, I was only fifteen minutes late from my (adjusted) ETA.

After Eniko, my new pal Lauren Tatner, whom I'd met just a month earlier at the past life regression intensive in the States, joined me for the night and for the workshop the next day. When I signed up for this workshop months earlier, I was going to be alone, staying at the workshop hotel, then leaving early Sunday morning. Now, I had three people to meet, Eniko, Lauren, and Mathew the next day. This was a regular press junket. The workshop almost became an afterthought.

Since I was beyond exhausted, Lauren offered to do Reiki energy healing on me. I gratefully accepted. I could feel the heat pouring off of her hands, the mark of a true healer. The session provided sweet relief. I felt refreshed, as if I'd just slept, or, well, been healed. We chatted a bit but I really wanted to cash in on the hot tub to further reverse the stress of the morning and the freezing cold air conditioning in our room.

The solarium was empty, a beautiful glass room exposing the blue sky above and the garden outside. The hot water, peace, quiet, sun and green vista (albeit with planes flying over low) was exactly what I needed.

Everything was perfect. The workshop was good, but the highlight really was the adventure itself, surviving the high drama of the first morning. I didn't chastise myself for not bringing my passport, that was a non-issue. In fact, the whole drama had a "meant to be" kind of core to it since it was an intentional "mistake" on my part, not an oversight. What really impressed me was how well I performed under extreme pressure. I stayed focused for hours and jumped successfully over every hurdle in my travel triathlon.

Meeting Mathew Hart for the first time was a pleasure, too. A fellow new ager and Facebook friend, we'd spoken on the phone and emailed here and there about spiritual stuff. He's in the film biz and related recent airport trauma of his own. Rushed during production of *Don't Breathe*, a movie he produced, Mathew traveled internationally while carting movie props, which included handcuffs and gun residue in a bag that had carried blank-shooting guns for the thriller still in production. Try explaining that to airport officials. Mathew missed his flight, too.

Lauren and I talked endlessly. She stayed in my room until midnight then headed home to her dog. I had a four a.m. wakeup call. I was going to take the four-thirty a.m. shuttle to the airport. Lauren gave me a few more minutes of divine Reiki healing, and I fell fast asleep. Sort of. I was on subconscious high alert so as not to make any more aeronautical errors.

I dreamt that my shuttle bus was full and I couldn't get on. Nervous, I woke up at three-thirty and bolted to catch the four-o-five shuttle instead (they run every twenty-five minutes!)

While waiting in the lobby, chatting with the lovely female night clerks, a gentleman rolled out a coffee cart and the gals told me that it was for people, like me, taking the shuttle. I felt so blessed. Caffeinated heaven in the dead of night.

A minute after pouring my brew the shuttle pulled up, so I hurriedly grabbed my bag, my luggage, and full cup of coffee. I hit the "door open" button with my foot via a roundhouse kick. The driver took my bag. *Finally*, the Great Wizard of Oz was ready to take me home. Expecting an empty van like the first time, I was shocked to see multiple faces staring at me in the very dim interior light. Adults and young kids looked at me expectantly. I felt like I had walked into a Jewish hiding place during the War.

"Who are you people?" I exclaimed. "Who travels in the middle of the night except crazy mileage people like me?" My dream (as they often are) had been prophetic, the bus was indeed packed, but, unlike my dream, at least I was able to get on.

Totally hyper, I grilled them. Though unrelated to each other, they were all from Toronto, and all on the same flight to Jamaica, except for one family headed to Orlando, Florida.

"Awesome kick," one dad observed. He had caught my roundhouse.

The ease with which I glided through Pearson Airport was remarkable. It was all so easy and effortless I looked around for more to do. I refused the horrible X-ray machine this time and received a most delightful pat down from a friendly female guard. Her touch was so light it almost felt like a massage. I wondered if they'd confiscate my leftover dinner that was to be my lunch later on. They didn't. Everything here was flowing, all systems go.

I loitered in the duty-free shop since I had plenty of time, AND a boarding pass. I treated myself to some dark chocolate. I hadn't spent any cash all weekend, and I was able to charge the bill in American dollars. More ease. I had left purgatory behind a long time ago. I was in Heaven now, all the way. With time on my hands, I chatted up the beautiful Indian saleswoman in the ice wine shop, Rajana, a single mom. We had a forty-five minute metaphysical talk and I showed her some ways to expand her own energy field.

Finally, it was time to board my plane. The ticket lady examined my passport and stopped short. She looked me in the eye, very grim, and handed my passport back to me. "I can't believe you got this far without anyone noticing."

My stomach gripped. I looked at her expectantly.

"You need to *sign* your passport."

Heck, everyone else was just glad I *had* a passport. And a boarding pass. On this flight, a missing signature was my worst transgression.

My return flight was on another small plane, and I had a seat toward the middle, on the aisle. The coffee was wonderful, all over again. My trip could not have been more perfect.

I repeated my public transportation route home from LaGuardia—$2.75 and easy as pie with smooth connections, like nothing had ever happened. But oh so much *had* happened, and all in less than forty-eight hours.

It wasn't until I got home that I noticed something on the back of one of my three boarding passes for my return flight. It was a note from the nice airline employee who (clearly) had been the one to help me get on board (it most certainly was not Gate Queen).

"All the best!!" wrote Airport Services Coordinator Donald G. Knight. My "Knight" in shining armor. You better believe Air Canada heard from me about how great he is.

The trip came in like a lion and went out like a lamb.

And since I believe in miracles, I think it's no accident that a man named "Peter" was there when things turned around for me and I finally received entry into Heaven, aka Gate A-5 at LaGuardia Airport. St. Peter is the Keeper of the Keys to The Kingdom, boarding passes, and free earbuds.

When I got home, I apologized to my cats for scaring the hell out of them then picked up my puppy from my neighbor who had taken brilliant care of all three heavenly creatures.

There's no place like home.

CHAPTER 12

Funeral For A Friend

The title of a tiny book in a storefront window jumped out at me as I strolled up the avenue. *All My Friends Are Dead*, it was called. What a delightful sentiment on a sunny day. *Who would buy that?* I thought as I kept walking.

Later, I caught up with a friend of mine over the phone, an older nun who lives in Houston, "I was at a funeral when you called yesterday," Sister Eileen said with her lilting Irish accent.

In all our years of friendship, she'd never mentioned attending a funeral.

That same day, I got an email from a Dead Friend. This is not the first time that's happened. Two years ago, I got a message from someone who'd died a few months earlier. The message was spam, but that's beside the point. She was communicating from the other side (Spirit loves electricity). I'd had a potent "lucid" dream about her, too, so I knew something was up. Spirit has many means of communication. Apparently, email is one of them.

EVP (Electronic Voice Phenomenon) is a form of

Spirit communication whereby a message is recorded on an electronic device (like voicemail, or a recorder). I wholeheartedly believe in the validity of this phenomenon, though I've not experienced it directly. Other phenomena—lights flickering, light bulbs exploding, appliances turning on, objects moving by themselves, and my finding very symbolic physical objects while out and about—I have experienced in spades.

This day, the email was from another Dead Friend's CaringBridge website, which documents a patient's journey through sickness and treatment so friends and family can be contacted en masse. In fact, the message was attributed to the deceased girl herself, which seemed a bit odd (though her parents did sign the note).

That night I saw *Woman in Gold* starring Helen Mirren. I was deeply moved by the story, having German Jewish ancestors myself, and was all the more moved because these relatives are all dead. Hearing this accent from my childhood, and seeing families, first happy, then torn apart, tore *me* apart. I was very maudlin and pensive when I walked home after the film.

In fact, I'd been feeling out of sorts, on and off, for the past few days—anxious, lonely, and restless—though I was able to reclaim peace again each evening.

The next morning, I glanced at emails before running off to the gym. My eyes fixated on "sad news." A friend had just died. A childhood friend I'd been communicating with almost daily for the last six months. Someone whom I'd known was gravely ill, but whom no one had any idea was at death's door. She "slipped out" shortly after the nurse checked her vitals in the morning.

People like to do that, die when no one's looking. It's easier that way. There's no one to hold you back. It's very hard to die when your loved ones are sitting there crying and desperately desiring for you to stay. It's also hard to die when a caregiver is there trying to keep you alive. Best to do it alone. And that's what most folks do. They slip out when no one's around, often in the middle of the night.

Interestingly, I lost two friends just ten weeks apart, both from cancer. One was forty-two years old and had eschewed all things medical, embracing nutrition and holistic healing until the very end when it became clear her approach had not done the trick. So, off to the hospital she went, but by then, that didn't help, either. The other was fifty-two years old and had embraced the medical establishment full throttle from the get go—chemo, radiation, transfusions, transplants—you name it, she did it. It wasn't until the end that she allowed in a little woo-woo stuff, a guided meditation over the phone from me, and Reiki energy healing from a local practitioner she claimed gave her great pain relief.

She'd had nuns praying for her (at my request), and Sister Eileen had sent her a copy of *Jesus Calling* (Actually a pretty cool book despite the silly title, she'd sent me a copy, too). I rolled my eyes at the title initially, but my friend, who was Jewish (though not religious) was even more astonished than I to be holding such a book. But when faced with death, you pull out the big guns, including praying nuns and Jesus books.

When I learned of my friend's death, my anxiety dissipated. Sadness and shock will do that to you. I wondered if I hadn't been empathetically feeling some of my almost dead friend's anxiety, or if it wasn't my own intuition about the impending event. Certainly there had been many signs pointing to this sorrowful and unexpected circumstance.

But not *all* my friends are dead. I mean, you're reading this, right?

I know both (dead) friends are fine. I know it's fun

and games Over There, all healing and roses and insight and upliftment. Yes, there's a panoramic life review (Judgment Day). You get to relive every second of your life in hyper speed but with full comprehension, recalling every thought and feeling you ever had, and (this is the panoramic part) you get to feel how everyone around you felt when you said and did all those crappy or amazing things. For additional insights into life in the beyond I can recommend *The Afterlife of Billy Fingers* by Annie Kagan, *Saved by the Light* by Dannion Brinkley, *Life After Life* by Raymond Moody, *Destiny of Souls* by Michael Newton, *Dying To Be Me* by Anita Moorjani, and Brian Weiss's many bestselling books, including *Only Love Is Real*.

There are "hospitals" on the other side. If you've been sick for a long time in the physical, you're energetically spent and need to recover. You need tender loving care, and you get it. You may not even discern that you're dead yet—especially if you don't believe in an afterlife—and you'll assume you're still physically alive because your consciousness has continued and you can't comprehend consciousness without physicality. This is what ghosts are. Energies who can't "give up the ghost" of their previous physical life for reasons ranging from obsession with drama and trauma (such as a violent death) or a low vibrational focus (a life filled with base feelings such as jealousy, hatred, revenge, rage, etc.).

But let's say you're a "good" person (happy, loving, emotionally healthy) who just doesn't believe in an afterlife. It may take such a soul a while to adjust to life outside of the body.

This soul (a friendly ghost) may hang around the earth realm because that's all it knows. But over time, the Higher Energies make themselves known to the basest or kindest of souls to lead them back home.

You figure it out, eventually. There is always help available.

For those who went through prolonged illness or trauma of some kind, the "Heavenly Hospital" provides an opportunity to recover from your exhaustion and your Earth-to-Heaven jet lag. When you revive, you have your life review and then discuss what's next. Learning continues on the other side. And your involvement with your loved ones in the physical continues, too. It's not constant contact (what would be the point of dying?), but the bonds of love never die.

Your loved ones are as close as a thought or feeling away. When you think of them, they know it, and can come to you energetically. There are windows to Earth from Nirvana. The realms are connected, and they can see us, just as some mediums can see them. The living/dead connection is similar to people living on different floors in the same high rise. They're united, even if in separate apartments. All you have to do is pick up a phone or ring a doorbell if you want connection. When you die, you get to be reunited with all your loved ones already on the other side.

Of course, if you were a tormented soul over here, it's a little harder when you're over there, because tormented folks just don't know how to have a good time anywhere. So, even when they're in a place of light, they create their own sandstorm (as they did on Earth). When they get tired of doing this to themselves (there's free will on the other side, too), they wake up to the fact that there is Love, Light, and Assistance (all euphemisms for God) available to them, the likes of which they may not have experienced in the lower realms (that would be Earth, not Hades). We make our Earth experience heaven or hell (and everything in between) based on our attitudes, beliefs, and choices.

Everyone has an expiration date. It's stamped somewhere, even though we can't see it. In fact, we have several potential exit dates, five, I believe, when we can opt out of our contract (yes, we all have contracts, with ourselves, essentially). There is a blueprint for our lives, and while some of the lines are carved in stone or written in ink, the bulk of life is for us to color in as we choose, with pencil, paint, or pen. We have free will. Our soul agrees to certain plot points for our growth and expansion before we incarnate, just like you pick courses in college. We choose everything in life, from the parents and circumstances we're born in to, to our physical bodies. This may not consciously make sense to you, but contemplate the power in that possibility. There is meaning in everything, even though it may remain hidden from your conscious mind.

Looking at both healing approaches of my two friends (one holistic, the other medical) what is one to conclude given the outcomes? I would argue that they both made the right choices for themselves, and that there is no one answer.

Life is the ultimate adventure park, encompassing thrills, chills, drama, romance, despair, conquest and loss. We buy our ticket, get on, and someday the ride comes to an end. But it's one ride of many. We come back over and over again, seeking new adventures, dramas and experiences, often with the same cast of characters, give or take a couple of replacements to mix things up. Love conquers all. It is the glue that keeps us together. It's the bond that connects us after death. It's a little trickier to communicate when one is in Spirit and the other is in 3D, but it's not impossible. You need to raise your vibration (by consciously evolving with greater clarity and focus) to connect with the higher realms, which vibrate at a higher pitch (which is why animals can sense Spirit in the same way that dogs hear a "silent" dog whistle, they are attuned to different frequencies). When you're in alignment with your inner self, you get frequent signs, as I do. When spirits wish to communicate, they have to lower (slow) their vibration to communicate with mediums or loved ones, while we have to "get up to speed," so to speak, to reach up to them.

It's good to remember that there is a Big Picture which we do not see, discern or understand until the "movie" of our life is over. But it's still there. There's a director and producer (our Soul and Guides). Despite the outline of our blueprint, no one knows how the story will end because we have free will (and can fail our courses, or exceed expectations). It's a good idea to embrace life and play our part to the hilt.

Another friend of mine just announced she is having her second baby at fifty-two. She had her first at fifty. Her sister-in-law's sudden death at fifty-one put fire in the belly of both she and her boyfriend and precipitated their decision to embrace life full force.

There are no answers. There is no right or wrong. There is only what works. And what you want. Be true to yourself and seize the day.

CHAPTER 13

On A Clear Day You Can See Forever

The young man was running for his life, an American soldier in the Vietnamese jungle, a killer breathing down his back. The long, terrifying chase ended with the young man's murder. Only the killer hadn't been Vietnamese. It was another American soldier. Tony saw something he shouldn't have seen, knew something someone didn't want him to know, and his killer saw to it that that information wouldn't be shared with anyone.

This was the past life memory of a young lady I took a weekend spiritual workshop with years ago. The trauma was vivid to her, as real as anything here and now. I don't remember if it came to her in dreams or visions, but they were recurring. She felt the terror, and she remembered her name in that lifetime. Tony. She had a date, too, 1967, presumably the year that Tony died. She was under thirty when I met her, and so had been reborn within ten years of Tony's death.

"Tony. You were Italian?"

Her answer surprised me. "I was black."

The person telling the story was a tiny American of

Japanese descent, a gentle, quiet, young woman who worked as a CPA in Washington, DC. Tony's physical type and personality could not have been more different from hers. I asked if she'd been to the Vietnam Memorial in Washington, the shiny, black basalt wall inscribed with the 58,300 names of the dead and the year they'd died. I figured she could probably find her full name if she looked for Anthonys that died in 1967. I believe she had visited the memorial, but hadn't looked for Tony.

She and I partnered up to do healings on each other during our workshop. I liked her a lot and never forgot her remarkable story.

I used to be petrified of fires when I was very young. Not of fire in general like The Monster was in *Young Frankenstein*, but of my apartment being on fire. I could see flames as I went to sleep. My mother added fuel to *that* fire by telling me that the more I worried about it, the more likely that I would attract the situation (yes, the law of attraction, thanks, Mom!). Needless to say, her warning only intensified my anxiety. I wasn't only afraid of fire, now I was afraid of my *fear* of fire, an invisible "accelerant."

It wasn't until years later when I was studying mediumship and psychic development that someone said she felt my entire family had been killed in a fire in a past life, and, as the only survivor, I had lost my mind from grief. That story resonated with me, and, later, I recalled my "irrational" fear of fire as a child. I've been devastated with grief in this life, and while I haven't lost anyone in a fire, or everyone all at once, I've lost the people closest to me when I was young (all four grandparents and both parents). I can imagine losing my mind from grief. I've almost lost it once or twice in this lifetime as it is. What's funny is that my mom and dad taught me to believe in reincarnation, yet Mom never tied my fear of fire and one or two other "imagined" traumas I shared with her, including a nightmare about my horse going over a cliff that left me sobbing inconsolably, with past life scenarios.

There's a TV show called *Ghost Inside My Child* about similarly dramatic recollections of past life traumas. It's particularly compelling because some of the stories from these very young kids (who are from one to three years old when the memories of the past life trauma begin) are verifiable. The kids, often toddlers, share sophisticated information about adult life they couldn't possibly know about.

The show's title is misleading and sensational because there's no ghost lurking. There's simply a past life memory in the child's consciousness. Once you start to expose and uproot the traumas of the past, phobias in this life related to the pain of the past tend to fade away. Hence the value of past life regression for many people.

Not all past life memories are traumatic. When a friend of mine in the theater's daughter was young, she startled her mom by chiding, "When I was *your* mother..."

I know one dog, one cat (both mine), and one human (both her former adult life and now her new life as a male toddler) who have reincarnated. It's fascinating to see the similarities, and the differences.

No one is identical the second (or hundredth) time around.

What's the point? The purpose of reincarnation is to gather new experience, not repeat the same old same old. Life is about growth and expansion, building up our knowledge base through new opportunities.

I spent five days at the Omega Institute in Rhinebeck, NY, studying with world-renowned psychiatrist and past life hypnotist Dr. Brian Weiss. He is Brooklyn born,

Yale Medical School trained, and was highly regarded in his field as a regular old shrink when one of his patients "turned" on him. Instead of regressing via hypnosis to earlier in this lifetime (they were trying to uncover the root of her severe phobia regarding water), she jumped tracks altogether and ended up in a different time, place, and body.

This was new terrain for Brian, but he went with it. What ensued was a series of experiences with this patient in past lifetimes, and in-between lifetimes when the soul reviews and plans its next foray into the physical with a team of guides. For a great overview of how some of this soul stuff works, watch the comedy *Defending Your Life* starring Meryl Streep. The information that came through this patient, including personal information about Dr. Weiss's private life (which she could not have possibly known), made it impossible for him not to contemplate reincarnation and the spiritual realms (which heretofore he had not considered) as credible. It is now the basis of his teaching and writing, and it is why I took the intensive with Brian and his wife Carole up at Omega Institute. He is a master teacher.

Prior to studying with Dr. Weiss, I'd had two very sketchy past life regressions, one took place decades ago, and the other a few years ago. Both times I was physically uncomfortable (The regressions took place in odd settings under even odder circumstances.)

When I shared that detail with Brian, he said, "You can stop right there."

Duh. If you're not relaxed, you can't be hypnotized. In both instances, I felt I had made up the stories, that I wasn't "really there" like some people seem to be when they're regressed and they relive traumas of the past. While I may have gleaned some insight into the past, I perceived things as an outsider, not an insider. I was hoping to have a more experiential sense of the past, like being dropped onto a movie set in full costume.

Hypnosis is not some weird trance where the hypnotist is in control. It is simply a state of deep physical relaxation combined with the participant's focused attention and openness to suggestions such as "You can now easily access memories from your childhood."

My class was filled with one hundred and fifty therapists, hypnotherapists, social workers, mediums, and healers, all enthralled with the man and his work. Brian has a very soft, gentle voice, eminently useful for relaxing folk. In fact, he induced us hypnotically so often that all he had to do was start talking and I'd go into an altered state. I was in just such a state for much of the time in class. My psychic abilities expanded, including clairvoyance (the ability to see beyond the physical).

We were there to develop our skills and to practice on one another. This way, we'd get to experience both being regressed and regressing others. Brian did several group regressions, but he also invited a few people (one at a time) up on stage to be regressed by him.

One was an adorable young lady from South America who claimed to have absolutely no memories of her early childhood.

Brian's manner was always comfortable and relaxed. After he induced her, she burst into an infectious giggle that alternated with boisterous laughter. Her giggles continued unabated except for occasional intakes of air and attempts to communicate.

"What's happening to you?" inquired the master hypnotist.

"My grandfather and mother are tickling me!" She burst into laughter again.

"How old are you?" he inquired.

"They're—changing my diaper!" Another spasm of laughter began.

Most everyone in class surrendered to her mirth and started laughing, too. So acute was her awareness as an infant that she knew her mother (clearly a single mom from the rest of the story) was very sad.

Brian brought another lady up on stage, someone who also had trouble being regressed (into past lives, not childhood). I closed my eyes as he induced her, and allowed myself to be induced concurrently. I heard what he was doing with her, how she was responding, yet had my own simultaneous regression. I had very clear visions of other places and times.

As well, I started seeing energy around people (auras). I saw a strip of bright light to the left of one woman's head. It was so strong I figured it had to be "real" so I directed my eyes out of "soft" focus to verify this. There was no light strip adjacent to the woman. My trip was all about "opening up." Whether regarding insights into past lives or increased psychic ability, spiritual energies are all connected. When you get one going, the rest will often follow.

For example, on the bus up to Rhinebeck, NY, I'd thought briefly of Mexican food, even though I wasn't hungry. I was tickled pink to find Mexican food for dinner in the dining hall, not because I love it (I do) but because I'd been gifted with a culinary psychic preview.

I also had repeated visions of two English sisters I'd met the summer before at Omega during trance mediumship class. I kept seeing them in front of their cabin, late at night, looking up at the stars in an area of the vast campus with which I was unfamiliar but had been exploring when I met up with them there that evening. My room ended up being in the same area as the English sisters' cabin.

Because I love to play with manifesting, I was hoping for a free upgrade to a private cabin (I'd paid for a dorm room). While I was not granted my wish, the Universe did me one better (this is why when you're praying, wishing, and manifesting, you always have to allow the Universe/God/Your Higher Self to add his/her finishing touches, as they often know better than you what would be best). I was put in a brand new dorm that was spacious, beautiful, and, pièce de résistance, had air conditioning. I was surprised to learn that many of the private cabins do not have A/C, and the first few days and nights I was there were hideously hot and humid.

My wish (really, just for a good housing experience) was granted. I even had Wi-Fi and didn't know it (just like Dorothy not knowing of her ruby slippers' power) until the third day of my visit, after lugging my laptop all over the place to catch the rare wisps of Wi-Fi on the campus.

When you are in right alignment with your soul's goals and your Deep Self, things start to go your way, and continue to get better as you increase your joy, passion, and sense of purpose. It's a snowball effect.

As you begin to open up spiritually, psychic gifts unfurl. And yes, there are people who are strongly psychic who are not particularly spiritual, but when I teach psychic development, the most important focus for me is always to work on personal development, happiness, and wholeness, for that is what fosters the blossoming of our "extra-sensory" abilities in a healthy and useful manner. These gifts are intended for good. Any ill use backfires on the sender (just as non-psychic bad deeds do).

There is nothing scary about ESP in itself, any more than seeing, hearing, or touching is alarming. In fact, I am always quite excited when expanded awareness becomes available to me. Or rather, when I become available to it, for when we quiet the mind and open the heart, miracles, even little ones, begin to happen.

Back in class, I discerned several past lifetime scenarios. When "remembering," it can feel like you're making stuff up, but that doesn't mean there's no truth to the visions. The impressions may seem like they're coming from your imagination, however, the part of you That Knows uses what feels like your imagination to plant information. Beware the left brain, which will relentlessly question and doubt. It likes to control things. And if you need to be in control, you can't relax, release, and have right brain, mystical experiences. When the logical mind interjects, "Yeah, but," just tell it to shut up. It's in the driver's seat enough of the time.

While I was in an altered state during class, I had a most unusual vision. At first, I saw our teacher, Brian, as a woman. It was just a brief glimpse of her face, and her energy. He does, in fact, have a fair bit of gentle, feminine energy. His wife is more overtly masculine in her expression of energy. Then a most astounding thing happened. The Lincoln Memorial appeared on stage big as life, and would not go away. I was mesmerized. As I stared and stared, the implication became clear. Our teacher had been Lincoln.

I happen to admire both brilliant men, one a lawyer, the other a doctor. Both love to talk non-stop, and to tell jokes. Both have helped to heal this country, and in Brian's case, the world. Both are diplomats (Brian handled two slightly uncomfortable situations in class with incredible aplomb and charm). Brian is even-tempered. According to his wife he is always calm. She implied that she's more reactive than he is. We all know how calm, cool, collected, diplomatic, and brilliant Lincoln was.

As with many cases, a soul's bodies in different lifetimes will resemble each other. Brian and Abe are both lean men, though Abe was taller. Both have full heads of hair, though Abe's never had a chance to turn gray (Brian's is white). They both have craggy faces with large noses, and small, deep-set eyes. Both their left eyes are bigger than their right. These are "markers," clues from the past.

His wife Carole even looks like Mary Lincoln, something Carole was not pleased about when I told her about my vision. I found a photo of Abe and Mary online that was almost identical to the catalogue photo of Brian and Carole.

"She was crazy!" Carole objected.

Brian made no comment, and when I asked if he'd ever had the awareness that he was Lincoln before, or if anyone else had seen it for him, he said no. Both the Lincolns and the Weisses were devastated by the loss of a beloved son. Carole mentioned in class that, as a younger therapist, she'd counseled many older, depressed women (something she'd found "depressing"). This would be an example of the soul trying to heal itself as Mary Lincoln *had* been emotionally and mentally disturbed (Who can blame her?). We are always helping ourselves, healing our past, present, and future through our interactions with other people and work on ourselves. Clearly both Brian and Carole Weiss have found great joy in this lifetime, with each other, their family, and with their work, which takes them around the world. The opportunity that physical life presents to all of us, through our various incarnations and lessons learned, is to get happier, wiser, and "bigger."

If you're interested in the spiritual wisdom available in between lives, I recommend Michael Newton's books. Newton is also a therapist/hypnotist, and while doing past life regression, found his clients talking between incarnations, as Brian Weiss had. The Soul (not the personality) revealed the bigger picture in fascinating detail. There is rhyme and reason to everything; nothing is random in a lifetime. Though we do have free will, the basic curriculum is set prior to birth in order to achieve balance and understanding based on what experiences and lessons are still missing from past lifetimes. Learning about the specific choices made to craft a lifetime before a soul takes human form is like taking a watch apart and examining the movement.

What were some of the lessons learned by my past life regression classmates? One woman recalled being a severely deformed baby boy abandoned at birth in another life. He was taken in at a monastery, loved unconditionally by the monks, and had a very happy life! He learned in that experience to "accept things exactly as they are."

This same woman also remembered two lifetimes where she didn't touch on a single aspect of the curriculum she had set out for herself beforehand. Her afterlife review included her grousing, "I can't believe I wasted *another whole life!"* which totally cracked me up.

Usually, it's "I can't believe I ate the whole thing." or "I should have had a V-8!" But no, these were entire *lifetimes* when essentially the personality (ego) chose just to live and not to learn. It's like going to school and doing no homework.

Another person shared that she'd recalled killing herself in a past life, and when she left her body, found herself laughing hysterically at the situation. I'd never heard of such a reaction to suicide. It struck me as weird but really refreshingly wonderful since suicide is always such a weighty topic.

Hey, it's her body, and she'll laugh if she wants to.

When a student expressed concern that patients might get "stuck" in hypnosis and not come back, Dr.

Weiss reaffirmed that this is impossible because hypnosis is simply a state of deep relaxation. He once had a patient who was resistant to come back so he used logic on her.

As he had another (very demanding) client coming in a few minutes, he whispered in her ear, "If you don't come out right now, I'm going to charge you for an extra hour."

She perked right up.

When back home, I regaled a friend with my experiences in class over the phone. He was seemingly fascinated then disappeared. I realized I'd been talking to myself for some time (not a new phenomenon). I tried calling him back, but his line was busy. Did the phone die? Did the connection drop? I finally concluded that I had bored him to tears.

He called me the next day to let me know my voice was so hypnotic that he fell asleep for several hours, the phone clutched in his hand.

CHAPTER 14

Food, Intuition, and Healing

How do you intuit what's right for your body? There are myriad advisories to consider and they often conflict: no gluten, dairy, meat, alcohol, caffeine, sugar, or soy. Yeast is out, but fermented is in (what?). It's easier to lose your mind than it is to lose weight, and weight loss is just one of many concerns for people trying to adjust their diet to improve their health. What's left to eat? A couple of beans and some wheatgrass.

Let me suggest this, other than avoiding things to which you have clear negative reactions, why not listen to your body and see what *it* says? I've been told to go gluten, dairy, alcohol, and caffeine free. Those are my four basic food groups (plus chocolate). All kidding aside, I eat a very healthy and moderate diet. Organic greens, vegetables, and fruits. Organic whole grains, often sprouted. Organic eggs. Olive oil, coconut oil, nuts. Meat. Organic dairy. Honey, maple syrup, and agave in limited amounts. Add to that a smattering of alcohol and caffeine. I refuse to feel bad about those choices, especially since I feel good. The proof is in the pudding.

As a kid, I had the tendency to be very obsessed with what I was eating, and became bulimic as a result. Any extreme is unnatural. I endeavor to buy organic as often as possible, but don't torment myself when I don't. A little poison won't kill you, and in this world, it's impossible to avoid all poison. We live in a dirty world. While it behooves us to clean up our environmental act ASAP, you can't freak out about how things are. You'll turn into a paranoid germaphobe, like Howard Hughes.

What *can* you abstain from? Torturing yourself about what you eat. You can eat the most "pure" diet possible (oh, say, non-stop organic wheatgrass juice) but if you live with fear, doubt, worry, and anger, all the health benefits of the greens will go out the window. You feed your body with your thoughts as surely as with your food.

A glass of wine lifts my spirits, as does moderate caffeine. I enjoy a square or two of dark chocolate daily. I have no obvious reactions to what I eat, so why should I stop? The whole idea of detoxifying makes no sense to me. It implies that I'm toxic, and I ain't. As well, if it's a temporary withdrawal, then you'll go back to "what's wrong" right after, so why bother? I resent the implication that I'm dirty and need cleaning. The modern obsession to purify, clean, detoxify, and de-germ borders on the puritanical (not to mention neurotic).

When I worked in publishing years ago, a colleague told me that she and her mom were amazed by the sludge that came out of them both when they had colonics. As I listened in horror, I thought about the piece of gum that I swallowed by mistake in fourth grade, and imagined a sort of Exxon Valdez spill lurking in my lower G.I. tract.

Surrounded at work by the Atkins all-protein diet book, *The Zone*, and *Sugar Busters*, I was making changes in my life. Cutting out carbs, sugar, and exercising more, I was enjoying a health and beauty renaissance. I decided to treat myself to something special, and since I'd already had facials but never a colonic, I sprang for the colonic, deciding to de-sludge once and for all. Turns out I was clean as a whistle. A lone bran flake came floating out, along with the gallons of water that had been pumped in. That was the last colonic I got.

When I told this to a new ager that I met recently, she affirmed that I was still dirty. "We all are." (She sounded like a damn Puritan). She said I needed to "dig deeper" and get another colonic. I guess I wasn't *trying* hard enough at my first session (I'm a sinner!) Contrary to her attempt to scare me, I trust the results of my first experience. I'm clean, and while it felt like a waste of money, at least I no longer harbor concerns about being filled with filth.

I spend my money on really good food now, more so than ever, and stand by everything I put in my mouth. It's an investment in my health. I'm proud of what I eat, and, most important, I enjoy it. Food is a terrific daily pleasure. Don't deprive yourself.

Over the years, I've become increasingly organic and whole grain. I eat more dark leafy greens, from mesclun to spinach to kale. I eat fewer sweets. And (this is a big one!) I have healthier human relationships in my life. Spend time with people who enhance your well-being and eschew the ones who don't honor your hopes, dreams, thoughts, and feelings. Bypass the bad (people, food, and circumstances) and invest in the good. Don't look for an overhaul or crash diet here. Incremental change is the best and most long lasting. Plus, your needs are always evolving.

A holistic approach to life means taking all areas of your life into account: physical, emotional, mental, and spiritual. They go hand in hand, and when you work on one, it impacts all others. But you can't ignore any of the four and expect to be balanced. It's like only studying math in school, with no English, history, athletics, or arts.

The body needs exercise. So move. Whether it's stretching at home, a walk in the woods, or jumping up and down like a lunatic on the sidewalk, do it. Need something gentle? Do Qi Gong or Tai Chi. Don't have time? Do something, *anything*, for five minutes. Ten sit-ups. Ten push-ups. Ten jumping jacks. Run around the bedroom in circles while you scream and wave your hands. Something is always better than nothing. Start small and build from there.

A friend of mine lost over a hundred pounds this year by making incremental changes. He improved his diet and started walking everywhere. He is now biking, something he'd never done before (he'd never owned a bike, not even as a kid). He looks and feels fantastic because he is feeding his body nutritious food and is giving it the exercise that it was denied for years. A dog needs exercise, play, fresh air, love, affection, and healthy food. So do you.

Don't look for the end result, just know that you're doing what feels right today, and you'll do what feels right tomorrow (which may be different). If you skip a day or a week, don't get mad at yourself. Maybe you need more sleep. Maybe you're upset about something and need to figure it out (remember, you can, if you listen to and honor your feelings). Take care of today's priorities and know that you're not going to fit it all in every day. Be flexible, forgiving, gentle, understanding, and compassionate with yourself.

Trust your gut. The more "sensitive" (intuitive) you become, the better you will know what your body wants to eat, what it wants to do, and who it wants to do it with. How many people do you spend time with out of obligation rather than desire? That's an example of "eating your greens" that will not benefit you. Seek out who and what feels good. Trust yourself.

Emotions need expressing. If you're angry, figure out why, and do something about it (no, not revenge, but correct the situation). Perhaps a friendship no longer serves you. Perhaps you need to speak up and set boundaries. Perhaps you need change in your life. It's up to you to figure it out and make the moves. If you're feeling love and joy, express that too! Don't keep it to yourself. Paint a picture, hug someone, say, "I love you." You can "be in love" all by yourself. You can be in love with life, and with you, and this constitutes a state of grace. Is that good for your health? You betcha. From time to time, try shifting your focus from "what can I get?" to "what can I give?" (which implies that you have it all) and see what happens. One attitude implies that you need love. The other, that you are love and that you can afford to spread it around.

Mentally, what are you feeding yourself? Do you read and watch dramas and thrillers, or, God forbid, the "news"? You are feeding yourself anxiety. Do yourself a favor and get rid of cable TV, like I did nine years ago. You can still view news online and rent stuff. Instead of watching hours of TV as most Americans do, you can read, meditate, listen to music, exercise, and be creative. You might want to nap. Dabble with coloring books as I have done for decades. It's a very Zen activity. Invite people over, talk, cook, relax, and interact. We get healthy by being happy and creatively engaged in life.

Spiritually, explore your beliefs. Do they feel good? Unless you have a higher perspective, it's easy to get lost in the mundane myopia of 3D. Lighten up and play more. Angels fly because they take themselves lightly.

Spirituality encompasses solitude, meditation, being in nature, playing, relaxing, and exploring mind-expanding thought. It creates a counter balance to the heaviness and rigidity of daily life. For we are not physical. We are energetic, vibrational creatures who don ever-changing bodies while we live as humans.

Life is change. Don't allow yourself to stagnate. Listen to your feelings, let yourself have fun, and enjoy your food!

CHAPTER 15

*Meditation for People Who
Don't Want to Meditate
(but are just a little bit curious)*

People think meditation is doing nothing, but it's not. It's active. Meditation is about focused discipline. But it's also about freedom.

Full disclosure right off the bat, I'm a terrible "formal" meditator. I'll look at the clock after one minute. Seriously. Sometimes I make it to three minutes, then I pass out (I do it before going to sleep, and upon waking up in the morning. Sometimes.) But I'm really amazing at freestyle meditation. Meditation my way. This I can do for fifteen to thirty minutes depending on the day. We're all wired differently. You, too, can discover "your way."

Once you have some insight into what meditation is, what it isn't, and learn a few tips and tools from me, you might be interested in dabbling yourself.

First of all, let's get one misconception out of the way. You can't turn off your thoughts. It's impossible. The only way to stop thinking is to die or get a lobotomy. Actually, when you die, your consciousness continues, it's just the brain that stops. Energy transforms but never disappears.

What you *can* do is tame your thoughts and choose the direction they go in.

Start simply by consistently choosing thoughts that feel good, also known as "daydreaming." Do this in your conscious life as well as in your "meditations." Feeling good is the key to health, peace, accomplishment, and enlightenment. Once you permit yourself to feel good, you can take those outrageous "daydreams" and allow them to simmer down into something more calm, peaceful, and more traditionally "meditative." But you don't want to break the bronco (i.e. your wild mind). In fact, you know that doesn't work. Can you *coerce* yourself into calm? I don't believe so. Taming anything benevolently requires wisdom and kindness.

Criticizing, judging, and berating yourself all lead to feeling bad, which is the very opposite of peace. It is this same "feeling bad" that creates all the discord, pain and violence in the world. When animals are in pain, they lash out. If people truly understood that being happy is the key to world peace (happy people don't go around hurting others, do they?) they would start to prioritize their own joy. It is not selfish to be happy, it is *essential* to our health. Learning to be happy is not the same as being narcissistic (narcissists are not happy people). Joy creates self-reliance, which fosters brilliance and creativity. You want to love yourself into harmony, which can transform into spiritual artistry. I'm talking about the path of least resistance, and that, my friends, is one of the secrets of life. Getting in the "flow" of life, instead of endlessly swimming upstream. *Feeling good is the key to it all.*

Why meditate in the first place? It's supposed to enhance one's general well-being. We want to add some calm to the "normal" crazy. Meditation is good at helping to reign in the "wild mind." Whether you're foaming at the mouth, frazzled by an overstuffed schedule, or just thinking crappy thoughts, it's good to take your mind to the cleaners from time to time.

So, sanitize your ruminations. Not just when you're meditating, but all the time. Examine your thoughts; don't let them spew out of your head willy-nilly. Thoughts have tremendous creative power and can either lift you up or tear you down. Do whatever you have to do to make your life more peaceful so that your "one-minute meditation" isn't the only time you achieve some serenity. You need to set the scene for the time when you actually *do* sit down to meditate. How can you make your life, home and job, more tranquil, and pleasurable? It's all about "style." Consciously set the tone in your life.

Invite peace in via warm baths and long naps. Diet from negativity. Change is an incremental process. Start small, and you will build momentum. You will get better at it, as will anything that is practiced regularly. Do you hang out with grumpy, cynical people? Or do you hang out with peppy types, maybe positive on the surface, but who bug the heck out of you? Do you do too much and run yourself ragged? Some people are afraid to be alone and to sit still, and as a result, burn themselves out with constant activity and chatter. If you're uncomfortable being alone, why? If you're unhappy sitting still, ask yourself why here, too. You *do* have the answers. Just dig a little. Be an investigative reporter and study yourself. Pull out a notebook and pen if you have to and have a conversation about "what's going on?" You'll be surprised with the results when you allow space for something to happen.

You're a fascinating creature. Take some time to appreciate yourself. It's like running your car into the ground instead of acknowledging how amazing it is to have a vehicle that takes you everywhere. Take stock of everything you have going for you, from your socks to your home to your sense of humor. You are an amazing person. If you don't think so yet, shift your attitude, and *make up* reasons why you're terrific. Play! It's all subjective, including the perception of "bad" things. Make stuff up that feels good. See what happens.

People associate meditation with austerity (just ask the Buddhists) but I don't. I equate it with pleasure. It's your meditation. You get to decide what it is. Meditation is focused thought. It's an invitation to make your life more "conscious." Since life is your creation, endeavor to make yours a masterpiece, not an afterthought.

How do you feel about silence? There is tremendous fullness in silence when you are at peace with yourself. Think of the sublime peace of the forest. Now, of course there are some sounds there, but natural sounds enhance our sense of peace and quiet. Nature feeds our peace and it's important to seek her out, any way you can. It's a little trickier in cities; however, it can be done. For urban types we have to create our own peace, a challenge to be sure given the frenetic energy we are enveloped by.

I chose to meditate this morning on the subway and, as I closed my eyes, I filled and surrounded my body with light. I then radiated light and love to everyone on my train, and afterward, had a pleasant conversation with a man standing near me. Even though I was running late, I experienced genuinely pleasant energy on this ride because I *produced* it. Meditation is an act of creation. And I arrived at my tap class right on time.

As a nature lover, I'm challenged by the omnipresent concrete of the city. Nature most assuredly feeds the soul and enhances our well-being. So where in the city can you find serenity? Museums, parks, tea salons, bookstores or boutiques (depending on the vibe). Just today I left Times Square and walked through four mini-parks with waterfalls in midtown Manhattan, and I basked in that soothing sound and energy for several minutes. (Falling water produces negative ions which make us feel positive. This includes the shower.) I take bike rides around the perimeter of Manhattan where I'm exposed to wind, water, and get to see the sky, not a common sight in a city crammed with skyscrapers. Frankly, Central Park has become too packed with people these days, however I still have a spot or two that remain sacred and silent. Churches and chapels are also very calming to me. Many are quite beautiful, and all of them are quiet.

Candles, incense, mood lighting, tea and soothing music create peace in my home. I don't have TV, and rarely keep my cell phone on. This sets the scene for when I meditate. It also sets the scene for my life. Ultimately, they can become interchangeable. Your life can become a "moving" meditation. This simply means you are living with consciousness, intentionality, and grace, which is the outward manifestation of peace.

I'm not suggesting you flush anger, sadness, grief, irritation, etc. down the toilet. Those unhappy feelings are not bad in and of themselves. They are simply indicators that something is not right in your life. It's your job to figure out what's "off" and do something about it (to the best of your ability).

Take stock of every aspect of your life. What do you feed your head? Nerve wracking "news," gossip, and extraneous information? Feed your head nutritious thoughts, such as "I'm okay. Things are getting better. I believe in myself." Kill the mental junk food, ("Life sucks!")

If you happen to be fixated on what's wrong with the world (I told you not to listen to the news!), you're definitely on a wild goose chase. Give that one right up (unless you've got tangible solutions and are acting on them). How many people spend time being angry about things they can't change, and, better yet, don't even bother to try? These people just grouse, grump, get ulcers, and, frankly, pollute the planet with even more negativity. Get right with yourself. Establish peace within, and you will help to create peace without.

This is about getting your own house in order. And if you accede my point that angry, disgruntled people only add to the world's problems (is there a better example of this than Donald Trump?) can you see that the converse is also true? Happy people anchor and amplify peace on the planet, by virtue of simply Being. Your vibration, your happiness quotient, your ever growing spiritual light truly helps this world. I'm not discouraging you if you're politically inclined, for taking action is key in life, but be mindful of the *attitude* you hold when you work toward your goals. "Fighting" for peace is an oxymoron. See if you can "keep the peace" even as you seek to grow it. Get Zen and contemplate "the movement in silence" and "the silence in movement." It's that Yin Yang thing.

Don't worry about always maintaining your Zen calm. Don't worry about being happy all the time. Our moods ebb and flow. Our thoughts change, like clouds moving across the sky, and our feelings reflect our thoughts. You never want to be rigid or static, and if you think of a body of water, sometimes wild, sometimes still, you'll understand that you are allowed those very same ebbs and flows. It's not about freezing the moment. Go with the flow, but do take responsibility for your behavior. As you get better at creating peace and happiness within, you'll be less rattled when you experience life's vicissitudes. You're building a "happiness muscle" with your inner work and you will eventually sail more easily, even over rough seas.

Do you have enough time alone? I spend a lot of time alone, and it suits me fine. There is often soothing music in the background when I'm home (Music is a vibration as surely as peace is.) I like being with people, too, but it's important to enjoy your own company. You're not alone. You're *with* you. The more comfortable you become with peace and quiet, the more you will feel the fullness of that silence. There's a lot there when you sink into it. But you need comfortable thoughts floating inside your head to feel relaxed. Thoughts create feelings. "I am calm" is a soothing thought. So is "all is well." The simplest of all is a mere, "I am." Make up some thoughts right now that feel good to you. These are mantras. Use them. Speak them out loud. You can make up more tomorrow as your needs change.

Imagine being in a beautiful forest (I love the forest. When you create your own scenario, you can go where you want.) I once instructed a mother and her young son that I was leading in meditation to pick a beautiful, natural setting. The five year-old felt compelled to blurt out where he went. Home Depot. That's his idea of heaven.

Anyway, you're in the forest and you have not a care in the world. Breathe in the fresh, clean air. Know that it is purifying your lungs and revivifying your body. The sound of water streaming from a distant waterfall and a babbling brook serve to further relax and rejuvenate you. The sky is blue, the sun is streaming through the green leaves, and you're blanketed in the serenity and magic of nature. Soft moss cushions your bare feet. You are at peace. You are free. You are safe. There's nowhere to go, nothing to do. Just revel in that feeling now. Take a deep breath. Smile. Stretch.

You just meditated.

You focused your mind on a particular topic, and that's all meditation is.

Some people stare at a candle flame, or focus on their inhalation and exhalation. Others repeat a mantra endlessly (that's my idea of losing your mind, but whatever works for you). Dorothy Gale (*The Wizard of Oz*) had a powerful mantra, and she only had to say it a few times: "There's no place like home, there's no place like home…" A visual focus (eyes open, looking at a flower or crystal), or a mental focus, either on your breath, a mantra, or pleasing image are simply tools to help you rein in wild thoughts. Another approach is to still the body and allow the mind to follow. Once you get the hang of it, you may not need the candle, the mantra, or the body to be in perfect stillness (you'll want to keep the breathing part going). Indeed, these tools can become crutches. We need to keep moving to continue growing. Even in stillness. We want active energy, not stagnation nor rigid, rote habit. Even a peaceful candle flame flickers.

I live the majority of my life in peace. That means that my days have become a moving "Valerie" meditation. Because I am focused and calm (most of the time), I can enjoy "moving meditation" even while preparing breakfast or cleaning the kitty litter. Coloring books or other hobbies are also a great way to focus and "lose yourself." Creativity aligns you with the "child's mind" where time and space (and bills and taxes) do not exist. Imagination, play, and desire expand into infinity, creating a mystical trance of sorts.

Synchronicities start happening when you spend time in this state of mind. Doors start opening for you where before they were shut. When you move through life with consciousness, gratitude and grace, not bumbling around as so many people do, you are in the process of becoming more peaceful, contemplative, and meditative. These qualities are conducive to a happy, relaxed and healthy life. That's the purpose of meditation anyway, to make you calmer, content, and ultimately, more productive and peaceful as you waste less energy being frazzled.

And don't think for a minute that I don't "let it rip" with loud music, wine, coffee, chocolate, laughter, racing on my bicycle or rollerblades, raucousness, and dance. Flip sides of the same coin. What good is calm if you don't also have celebration? Remember, we're not looking to get a lobotomy here. We're looking to have a good, happy, healthy, joyful, loving, creative and fulfilling life. Right? The same Spirit that created babbling brooks also created thunderstorms and earthquakes. We are fire and rain, peace and paradise.

Focus on what makes you happy. Eschew that which does not support your peace and well-being. It can be done. You may not be an island, but you can be selective. Curate your life.

Once in a while, try sitting down, taking some deep breaths, smiling, and see what happens when you close your eyes. Let yourself daydream, even with your eyes open. There are no rules here, so make up your own. Empower yourself with that thought.

Think of pleasant things. You may be surprised at how much time passes when you are having quiet fun, with or without coloring books, contemplative cooking, or meditative quilting circles. Time and space disappear. Get lost in the activity, in active, conscious, focused thought. This is meditation. See where it takes you. For while you may initially hold the reins, you may be surprised by Who and What takes over. It can become a magic carpet ride. Let your mind be blown. Allow space for the unknown and be carried away.

CHAPTER 16

GOING DEEP: Mining the Gold Within

I received a warning from Spirit, a threat, if you will, that I needed to up the ante regarding my meditation "practice" (which was a hobby at best). I'd received channeled messages from On High for decades about the value in my meditating daily. You know, like *seriously* meditating, not the way I had been—sometimes for a minute, sometimes for twenty, and sometimes not for weeks.

Spirit pulled out the big guns and pointed them right at my head.

I needed help with something specific and had asked a question, but they weren't going to give an inch unless I paid up first.

I had dabbled with meditation for years. I even took a class, but fell asleep in the darkened room until I was awakened by a bang. It was my forehead hitting the school desk I was seated at. Or was that automatic writing class? At any rate, my days of meditating recreationally were over.

I was at yet another standstill in my life, financially, socially, you name the category—on the surface, things were dead. Impatient for change, I was told the change would come from within, only when I meditated.

"Nothing will move in your life until you meditate longer and with regularity. This is the only way your Higher Self can get your attention," my pal Nicole said.

They were done with hinting and suggesting to their recalcitrant ward. Instead, they held my life ransom. I guess even God has Her limits when she's got an agenda that needs attending to.

I've been threatened by Spirit before. While many people think God wants us to "behave," I'd once been admonished by Spirit to become sexually active. I was too old to be on the shelf. Depressed over the death of my second parent in my early twenties, I just wasn't feeling jiggy. The message from Spirit went roughly: "It almost doesn't matter who, what, when, or where, but you have to do *something* with *someone*, for God's sake. Don't sit around waiting for the love of your life." Which I was.

This is the very reason I have to start smoking each New Years. I live alone and work at home. My eighty-year-old nun pal in Houston, Sister Eileen, has a more active social life than I do, taking three meals a day with other people, for starters. I'm so squeaky clean (save for cussing and drinking) that I have nothing to give up.

Except not-meditating.

Well, I took this threat from Spirit as a real challenge. "You want me to meditate? God damn it, I'll meditate!"

I sat down that very day and did something I'd never done before. I meditated for nearly three hours. Not all at once. I did it in three separate sessions. But I did it. I fucking did it.

I could hear the spirits cheer "Hallelujah" when I finished my final session late that night.

And yes, after decades of ignoring their pleas for me

to hunker down and "sit," I felt very accomplished having finally "sat," as if I'd just run a marathon. Even though I just sat on my ass.

Spirit knows how to throw its weight around with me. I pull cards from various tarot type decks every morning. There's an angel card (or some shit) from one deck or another that admonishes *GOD IS IN CHARGE*. Whenever I pull it, I grumble, "Jeez, what a control freak! All right, God, knock yourself out. *Be* in charge. You're so *damn* pushy!"

(Don't worry about blasphemy. God appreciates my perky personality.)

The fact is, there are things that are out of our control and things (when fate pounds on our door) that behoove us to confront. Even activities as simple as doing the dishes, laundry, or vacuuming. We may not particularly want to do them, but when we do, we feel better. We restore order to chaos. And we don't smell.

When I finally face the music, these undesirable invitations inevitably produce transformation, despite my preliminary fear, trepidation, resentment, heel-dragging, and cussing. On the day I asked Spirit when things would change for me, God played the Mafioso. A black car pulled up. A door opened, a gun was waved. "Get in the back."

Given my need for help, I was in no position to argue. I went along for the ride. I was good and sober when they threw me out of the car. They meant business.

So what happened when I took my marching orders and started to meditate in earnest?

It was interesting.

Exhilarating.

A wave of experiences washed over and through me.

I worked through all those little things you'd expect, like restlessness, boredom, discomfort, thoughts like

"This isn't working," "I have to blow my nose," "I gotta pee," "My nose itches." And so on. And you know how I dealt with them? I went to the bathroom, blew my nose, and scratched when necessary. I'm not into suffering. I'm not an ascetic. And I don't believe denial is the path to heaven, enlightenment, higher dimensions, or higher consciousness.

Transcendence is not about killing our human aspect, or the ego. It's about taming it. Civilizing it. Incorporating it into the bigger, non-physical aspect of ourselves—consciously connecting the human to the divine, effecting a powerful weave of the two.

Once I addressed the issues of my nose and bladder, I hunkered back down to hook up with the higher dimensions.

Determined, I kept at this meditation thing thrice daily. Spirit gave me a challenge, and I accepted. I sat and sat and sat some more. And I got somewhere. I really did. I started to experience different sensations, different states of consciousness. Some were ecstatic. Some were peaceful. Some phases even seemed "thoughtless," "empty," or "mindless," something I had deemed impossible. I know now it's possible to still the lower mind, and I won't qualify it, other than to say it's a mystical experience and you'll see for yourself when you get there.

Time started to fly, then it disappeared altogether. I enjoyed being alone in my soundproofed work studio, my top priority to be with myself and to open up to higher states of being (perhaps the way other people approach using recreational drugs). All the anxiety of needing to do, to get, to prove, to change, to fix, to produce, to procure, went out the window. My only desired connection was to Me. I was the experiment, the archeologist, and excavation site, peeling away layers of my persona and the contrived construct of our "reality."

I kept this up every day.

I felt accomplished. More peaceful and content. Happier.

I was going places while going nowhere at all.

I even purchased a magic carpet (a purple meditation pad and pillow) to enhance my travels.

While meditating, I allowed myself to play. I started thinking happy thoughts. My goal was never to still the mind, it was simply to "go within" and engage myself on a deeper level. I indulged in daydreaming and creative visualization. My varieties of experience were very much like watching clouds drift by. I both allowed and created, engaging with the shifting energies. There were moments of bliss.

Whereas, previously, I had looked elsewhere and outside for things to do, suddenly I was the activity. I had a date with myself, three times a day, and I did this religiously for at least a week. The hunger for more outside was gone. My questing was now internal.

I also experienced physical and energetic sensations, tingling in the palms of my hands, heat in my body, tingling in my third eye and head generally. This is the good stuff, when you know circuits are firing and that psychic and spiritual energy is being activated and moved. I was building my internal fire.

Within a week, I booked a job, my first audio book narration in almost a year. Spirit was true to its word.

Then more audio book recording work poured in, time returned, and the clock started ticking again. My peace flew out the window as I booked job after job. My breathing became shallow and anxiety returned, the compulsion to audition for more jobs and to complete the ones I had creating mounting stress. I realized I had to figure out a way to meld both worlds, the one of productivity, the other of being.

When I first started recording audio books a few years ago, two of my pets had just died back to back. My grief was profound, and I worked long and hard at the computer to distract from it. I was so stressed that I fell apart (carpal tunnel, compromised eyesight, back and shoulder pain, massive ear infections that distended my head, and a thyroid condition). When I stopped booking jobs, I was relieved. I needed to recover. But then, I needed income.

So, this was round two of recording books. I was an experienced narrator and producer by now. I had more pets. And I had new meditating skills. I was determined not to stress myself again into sickness and despair.

I know that being healthy and happy is as important as finding right livelihood and being productive. I had to create the proper balance between the two, between being and doing. But I wasn't going to take an hour off to just "sit," not now that I had ants in my pants with so much work to do. Performing and producing felt diametrically opposed to just being. Additionally, when I'm recording, I don't write. That's a different frequency as well. In fact, writing is a form of meditation for me. Receiving ideas from the ethers requires being open to them. It is both active and receptive, the very way I experience meditation.

While I wasn't meditating as long and hard as I'd initially done to prove my mettle to Spirit, I was still dabbling, and I knew this was okay (I'm not a Rules Girl). I also wasn't working as long and hard as I'd done the last time I made myself sick from stress. I was pacing myself. Those were magic words. I'd stop. Take a walk with my dog. Have a cup of tea. Stretch. I couldn't work as hard as I'd done before. That way lay madness.

I completed all my recording work and decided to enjoy my freedom, to start meditating in earnest again, and to write. That's when another recording project came in. Sigh. I couldn't stop the press. I needed the work, and life is not all or nothing. So, yet again, I had the opportunity to weave the two worlds together and figure out some kind of comfortable flow between being and doing. I worked even *more* slowly this time (it was one audio book, vs. six projects, or fourteen, as I once had simultaneously). In other words, I was becoming more mindful and centered while in the midst of my activities. That's the sweet spot.

I'm finessing my Zen calm. For instance, when there are interruptions or noises as I'm recording (they are legion), I don't get as upset as I used to and find I'm able to remain neutral at times, and, better yet, sometimes even smile or laugh about the disturbances. These are the benefits of meditating regularly (and a healthier solution than psych meds). You go within to your ever-present center of peace and calm, and come out refreshed. It's your very own isolation tank, full night of sleep, walk in the woods, super food smoothie (or double espresso—whatever makes you happy.)

When we're calm and centered, we can weave through dimensions like we weave through traffic. Learning to go from high-stress human-mode to peaceful meditation-mode is not unlike shifting gears when you drive, learning to upshift and downshift from the higher realms, and not become derailed altogether when you get in an accident, stuck in traffic, or barely escape a scrape. As you deepen your practice, you will adapt more quickly to the shifts. There is an acclimation period as we meld the human and the divine aspects of ourselves, but it's no different from getting out of the water after swimming, or cooling down after a long run. The more frequently and deeply we connect with our eternal aspects, the easier it is to be Human.

Flexibility is the key to success. If you can't meditate one day, don't beat yourself up. Some days you don't get enough sleep, or any exercise. The more accepting you are of your changing needs and life's fluctuations, the easier it is to get back on track.

If you're just not in the mood, don't do something. Honor your feelings. Yet sometimes if you simply nudge yourself (to meditate, clear your desk, do your taxes, do the dishes) you can move through the activity into a place of peace (not to mention a sense of accomplishment). The more you get in alignment with yourself, and work *with* your moods, the more your life will begin to flow easily and effortlessly. See if you can take things (and yourself) less seriously.

If you're feeling stressed, slow down. No, stop, altogether and take stock of yourself. Walk out of the room to clear your head. Take a nap. Take a shower. Take a walk. Listen to music. Shed a tear if you have to. Stretch. Have tea. Coffee. A glass of wine. Meditate. There's no right or wrong answer. *Trust your wanting.* Remember, you're in charge.

We need a balance of rest, play, work, time with others and time alone. It's never the same percentage each day. Things are always shifting, morphing and moving, even when they seem still.

As I go deeper and higher in meditation, I still experience challenges in my personal life. Meditation and spiritual growth don't make your problems go away. Your practice will dredge up issues in order to further clear your plate. Now that you're revving your engine, what are you going to do with your Zen skills? You're going to race the Indy 500. Challenge is the medium in which personal growth is cultured. As your core strengthens, road blocks that seemed insurmountable turn into gentle speed bumps. And speed bumps are good, because they remind us fast-paced lunatics to slow down.

Contemplate that there is an energetic team within and around you ready to serve your needs. We all have an etheric entourage, but they cannot help us unless we solicit their guidance. There is gold within, but you have to *actively* mine it. It starts with your intention, it continues with your will, and comes to completion with your follow-through. Persist.

Think of the Dalai Lama's bright energy, his endless enthusiasm, his frequent laughter. They do not diminish the fact that the man works hard and travels frequently. He's old. His country has been devastated by the Chinese, his gentle friends and countrymen murdered, his sacred temples destroyed. Of course it weighs on him. But he is resilient.

The stronger a connection I create with Spirit and my Self, the more power and endurance I have to deal with the visible world of conflict, chaos, contrast and challenge.

There's a saying, "Before enlightenment, chop wood, carry water. After enlightenment, chop wood, carry water." *The world doesn't change. You change.* As you do, your experience of the world changes, and the world responds to your transformation. Nothing exemplifies this better than Bill Murray's character Phil in the movie *Groundhog Day*. Same shit, different day. Rinse, repeat. Life is just one boring humdrum hollow non-event for cynical Phil. He keeps hitting his head against the wall with his cranky, pessimistic, selfish attitude, and it keeps slapping him in the ass. When he starts to play with life, approaching it like an experiment instead of a punishment, he engages himself passionately in the world. By taking piano lessons, helping others, participating in social events, by truly *living*, he becomes happy, fulfilled, and a hero. *The Phantom Tollbooth* by Norton Juster also outlines this profound process, in the guise of a (very sophisticated, adult friendly) "children's book."

As I continue to ace my tests, life becomes easier and better by the day. Challenges fall by the wayside, for they're not there to punish you. They're there to *grow* you. I still walk into rooms and find that, for instance, the cat is eating my duvet (aided and abetted by her sister who ripped the thing open, liberating the feather feast in the first place). Instead of overreacting, I interrupted the banquet and proceeded to repair the duvet.

Not unlike other humans, my challenges have been legion, from work to money, health and social relationships, you name it. However, my ability to bounce back to a happy or comfortable place, to have perspective, to not get upset or as engaged in drama as I used to, is greater due to the fact that I am regularly entering the higher realms and forging powerful alliances there. Think of your meditation practice as a secret garden, an inner sanctum, a country cottage, or your own private island.

As gentle as those images are, going within is also ninja boot camp. This is not sissy work, for sure. How many people do you know who can disconnect from the modern frequency of stress and ADHD techno-distraction and maintain even a *moment* of eye contact with another human being, let alone achieve inner peace and physical stillness for fifteen minutes? The effort is monumental to gain this particular control of self, particularly in this day and age. The results are also monumental. Forget guns and weapons of mass destruction. *This* is warrior training. Become a Master of your Self. Make the shift to peace, personal power and sovereignty. That level of mastery produces a Neo at the end of *The Matrix*. There's a reason that film was so popular. It touches an understanding within us regarding our own potential. But who out there is achieving it?

When we get into the flow of life, the machine starts working optimally. Meditation is one of the most powerful ways we can lubricate our divine motor works. It revs the engine and raises our vibration so we can forge our human and divine selves into a dynamic partnership. Our Soul, our Higher Self is simply a piece of God. A chip off the old block. It's Us in Higher Vibrational Format. Consider the spectrum of light, some of which is invisible. The Human Self is at one end of the spectrum, the Divine at the other. However, they are connected.

I've been on a conscious spiritual path my whole life, but as I up the ante by doing the inner work (which includes but is not limited to meditation) my psychic abilities have increased. I receive myriad signs, symbols and synchronicities on a daily basis, and it is a sheer pleasure to have the Universe interact with me in this playful and empowering manner. It's because I've gone "online." I invited and activated the connection. You have to earnestly engage.

A few short examples. I was in the post office on April twenty-first. As I was leaving, at eleven-thirty a.m., I looked down to see a red Fender guitar pick on the ground. I picked it up and contemplated it. Why would I find this? I've dated a few guitar players. My mind scrolled through that Rolodex and settled on a fellow who once toured with Prince. I put the pick in my change purse, walked away, and let the thought go. Two hours later, I learned that Prince was dead. Yeah, I know, the pick should have been purple.

I dreamt of a pair of shoes belonging to a friend of mine who passed away this year. When I checked my emails shortly after waking, I discovered her husband had organized a walk in her memory.

I wrote a friend last week and, when I didn't hear back from her, wondered what was up. I dreamt about her this morning. She was speed-walking through a tunnel to get to me. When I checked email this morning, she had finally written back. These are small things, but they are accurate reflections of or predictions regarding my waking state, and I enjoy the heads up from the inner realm about my connection to both worlds.

And finally, a slightly bigger and more amusing example of how the Universe plays with us when we're game.

While hunkering down to meditate, I employed a technique I'd read about and was intrigued by. I invoked the words "Reveal Thyself" to whoever was listening, working with me, and encouraging my spiritual growth. I'm not naming names.

I wanted to up the ante. For while I can relax, center, and reach higher, deeper states of consciousness while meditating, I was hungry for more. I wanted some flash, some pizzazz, you know, some psychic phenomena, like a vision, or a message I could hear. It was Friday night. I wanted fireworks.

While seated in meditation in a dark room I spoke the words aloud, "Reveal thyself to me. Show your face. Go on, make yourself useful!"

No sooner had the words been spoken than my room became ablaze with light. So brilliant was this radiance that it stunned me out of my reverie. Talk about "Ask and it is given." The response was *immediate*. What the heck was going on? Was there a burning bush in the middle of the room? My eyes popped open to witness my wall of windows illuminated by a blinding light so intense it could have emanated from a spaceship preparing to pick me up. I was peacefully meditating, asking for a stronger connection with higher dimensions, when God switched the lights on. "Surprise!" The room was electrified. God doesn't mess around.

I must add that these windows haven't been washed in so long that Zero Mostel's line from Mel Brooks's 1968 film *The Producers* comes to mind when I look at them, "Window's so dirty you can't tell if it's day or night." He tosses some of the black coffee he's drinking onto the glass to "clean it" then casually swipes the grimy mess with his tie.

I don't clean my windows often because I live on a busy thoroughfare in Manhattan and as soon as I clean them, soot reappears instantly. Cleaning the windows in NYC is an uphill battle that I gave up long ago, or like Erma Bombeck said, "Cleaning the house while you have kids is like shoveling the walk while it's still snowing."

Despite the grime, this UFO, or my Higher Self, was able to pierce the crud with its searchlight.

I leaped up and jumped to the window to see what was going on out there. A light shone from the main thoroughfare near me, a big cross street in Manhattan, high up on a crane. My first thought was that they were making a movie. But why would they be shining the light into my apartment? Were they filming me?

The light swiveled. Perhaps they were doing roadwork? (a constant in this city). I was curious to find out what was going on. I grabbed my dog and went to see who was responsible for this "act of God."

The Good Wife was shooting down the block. I spoke with a production assistant, a young man who meditates himself, and appreciated my humorous account of asking for "more" from Spirit and receiving it via network TV. I then chatted with the two gaffers operating the crane that had temporarily focused on my apartment and asked how many watts were required to light up the night sky. Eighteen thousand.

The following day, I went to Central Park with my dog. We bumped into an adorable but cynical neighbor who had just been in the park and she warned, "It's filled with assholes."

Milo and I waded through hordes of selfie-taking shopaholic tourists in the park. A little boy lunged to grab my puppy, who bolted in terror.

I blurted, "Don't chase my dog!"

His grandma defended the little terror by lying. "It wasn't intentional. He tripped!"

We passed a couple who just got engaged and a couple of bridal parties taking photos. A ballerina en pointe posed for photos by Bethesda Fountain. A mostly toothless older Latino man, who wore torn fishnets and chipped nail polish, waved amiably at me. I waved enthusiastically back.

It wasn't until our walk in the park was coming to a close that I realized the full impact of the Burning Bush/UFO incident the day prior. Milo and I were descending a steep set of stone stairs that led from a wooden gazebo atop a mountainous hill when the light bulb went on.

I had asked Spirit to reveal itself. Eighteen thousand watts lit up my room, making it feel like a direct call and response in church. I asked, and it was given. Yet, what was revealed? Despite my dirty windows and because of my lack of window treatments, *I* was revealed. I was exposed, as surely as if I were center stage in a spotlight. *I am The One I Am looking for.*

Like everybody else, I look for God and answers and messages outside of myself and keep forgetting what I believe. I am God. We are all God. Each and every one of us is an expression of the Divine, whether or not we know it or behave in divine manner. I *know* this, and yet keep acting like a putz who needs help from a psychic hotline.

Which is why Spirit told me to stop and meditate *se-*

riously. Because this is when you discover the meaning of, "Be Still, and Know that I Am God." When you are still and self-contained, you remember Who You Are. *You* are the woman or man behind the curtain, the great and powerful Wizardress or Wizard of Oz. *Do* pay attention to Her!

The nature of consciousness is never ending expansion and transformation. God likes to stretch, explore, and even to party. What do you think geysers and waterfalls are doing? They're having a blast. The more we step into our Divine Shoes, the more fun our lives become.

Meditation is not nothing, any more than outer space is empty. There are infinite worlds within, just as there are myriad worlds without. The bible quote "In my father's house are many mansions" refers to these many dimensions, or levels of consciousness. Close your eyes and See.

CHAPTER 17

BEGINNINGS
Or The Land of the Purple Glove

I'm losing three people from my home front. Two neighbors—including Shirley, whom I've known since I was nine and with whom I'm quite close—are moving to senior housing. Additionally, my building's warm and wonderful superintendent of fifteen years is leaving. The impending changes were revealed to me within days of each other and are occurring back to back. While no one has died, their departures feel like a death. It's the end of an era, and I feel left behind.

Within four months Vanity, fifty-seven; Bowie, sixty-nine; and Prince, fifty-seven, died. Shocking and sad for many of us (though probably not for my senior neighbors or Irish superintendent).

I grew up with Bowie, Vanity, and Prince, the latter two boosting my burgeoning sense of sexuality. The announcement of their three deaths, along with my three friends' imminent departures threw me for a loop. Why do things like this come in threes? Why does change sometimes happen all at once? Beats me.

After I cried, I decided that their change was my

change, too. If new things were coming to them, then new things were coming to me, too. Every death is a rebirth. Whether we perceive it, life is constantly renewing itself. Nothing is static. The weather shifts. Our cells die, new cells are born. We crave stability and security and put locks on our homes and even decorate our pocketbooks with gilded clamps. But you can't lock out change. It is the very nature of life. So why are we so resistant to it?

In short order, I was able to turn a dour mood around for myself. Mind you, in the distant past, when my mother got sick with cancer and died from it, I was not able to turn it around. I was depressed for years, and experienced significant grief before and after her death to boot. But I persevered, forged ahead, and have become emotionally resilient.

Since I want change in my own life on many frontiers, I'm metaphorically packing my bags. Cleaning house. Cleaning up. Getting my affairs and papers in order. I'm preparing.

This is where my hard work over the years has paid off. When you've processed your emotions, thoughts, and issues, you clean the slate to make way for the new. You can't do that if you haven't worked through your stuff. You just bring your baggage with you. But I've worked long and hard to become happier, freer, and am primed to move toward new vistas. Change is here.

For one, I am increasingly psychic, and this is a great and good thing. I've learned to trust myself, and have turned inward for answers instead of following the modern fixation of seeking relief from a pill, expert, partner, activity, job, or family to fill the voids and create one's sense of identity. This has connected me to my own powerful core.

I have taken the recent "deaths" and turned them into

my rebirth. For starters, I'm burning birthday candles. Shirley gave me her stash of yahrtzeit candles, tea lights, and other assorted candles she kept around in case of a blackout, including birthday cake candles in a decomposing box marked "Ten Cents" (what century were *those* from?)

It's still cold in New York, even though it's May, and I need their warmth. Candles instill a great sense of peace in me. I'm burning all of them, including her memorial yahrzeit candles for the dead. Birthday and memorial lights burn simultaneously.

I have a forest of candles around me now as I write. I light the tiny birthday candles one after another like I'm chain smoking. There's no cake. They're on a small metal plate. I light the new wick from the old candle burning down, then melt the new one's bottom so it adheres to the dish. I'm burning them all to cut down on clutter. Besides, who wants hundred-year-old candles on an actual cake? This bonfire warms my soul.

I'll give you examples of what blossoming psychic ability looks like. One morning I thought of an old friend I've been out of touch with. She wrote me that night to say her uncle died that morning.

I noticed I was missing an earring right before I was to lead a private session with a client. I concentrated on where I could have lost it, came to a conclusion regarding it's probable whereabouts (in a park a block away), then made a mad dash in the ten minutes I had left to go find it. It was buried in dirt, but I found it, and made it back in time for my appointment. You could argue that I used logical discernment, but once I did, I "knew" where it was and lickety-split retrieved it. My intuitive vision is focused like a laser beam. I'm psychically "online."

A few months ago I lost a purple chenille glove in Central Park when I was with my dog. Aside from the lost earring (which was pulled from my ear by a big, roughhousing puppy, unnoticed by me at the time), I'm not a person who loses things. But somewhere along our three-hour walk spanning several miles, I dropped a glove.

Disappointed, I backtracked a bit. In the past, I might have backtracked all the way home. But I have a looser grip on life now, and after ten minutes, I let it go to the best of my ability. I put the remaining glove in a bag for charity. There's another Michael Jackson out there somewhere who's gonna love it.

The next day Milo (my pooch) and I went to the park again. Since we generally follow the same route, I lightheartedly set the intention to find my missing glove, despite the fact that Central Park is 843 acres. Why not? Setting intentions is a way of playing with the Universe, and discovering your own co-creative abilities. When we got to the park, I joked to Milo "Go fetch my glove!" He didn't.

I did. I found it in the middle of a green field, an ultraviolet chenille flower lying perfectly preserved from the day before. This is a field perpetually filled with people, picnics, and dogs. Heck, a squirrel could have grabbed it to pad his nest within the past twenty-four hours. But there was no one around on this beautiful day. The glove was waiting for me, untouched. I glowed. The find was symbolic and inspired a new mantra: "I am a person who finds things."

In fact, I was never someone who lost things. Until lately, when I've been losing things left, right, and center (I still haven't found my umbrella). I made this perspective up: the reason I've been losing is to show myself just how well I retrieve. I'm a psychic detective.

The stakes were raised when I lost my iPhone. I was at an all-day class in the Wall Street area on a Saturday, took a walk during lunch, put it in my bag, and when I got back to class...gone.

I ripped my bag apart to no avail. The ramifications of the loss hit me hard. Was I still under contract with Verizon? (Yes. They own me for another year). I would have to buy another phone at full price (the cost of a car). I couldn't contemplate that, so my mind started looking for solutions. Was it stolen? Did I drop it? Could I find it? *I'm so damn good at finding things, I'll just go find my phone!* Wall Street is pretty quiet on the weekend. The phone's bright red cover would make it easy to spot, and I could easily retrace the steps of my short walk. But there were two more hours of class left and I just couldn't concentrate for the life of me with the issue unresolved.

So I took action. I walked to the front desk and asked if anyone had turned in a red iPhone. No. Would he call the downstairs guard and ask him? I waited while he called. No go. I asked to use his desk phone to call Apple Care. Apple was useless. "For security reasons" they wouldn't help me, the actual *owner*. If banks can establish security questions to determine that I am who I say I am, so can Apple, for Christ's sake. It's my phone. I've paid Apple very good money over the years, and, when push comes to shove, they told me to find someone with an iPhone to find my iPhone. Thanks for nothing.

Who had an iPhone? I recalled that a girl was using her MacBook Air in my class that day. Bingo. I approached her quietly during class and asked if I could use it. She offered me her iPhone instead. It located my iPhone, all right. It was on the move. My stomach dropped. Someone had found it. I could watch it walking along Broome Street in Soho. Was it having a good time?

Then, an uplifting thought dawned on me. What if the people who'd found it were returning it to the Apple store on Prince Street? Wouldn't that be wonderful? I expect miracles. That would be a miracle! Then my thoughts started roaming again, like my lost phone. If they'd stolen it (how, I don't know), would the thieves be shopping in Soho (a pricey neighborhood)? All bets were off. With my classmate's app I commanded my phone's automated message to display: "This phone has been lost. Please call..." I entered my home phone number. Having done everything I could logically do, I settled down and was able to pay attention for the rest of class.

When class ended, I ran to call my home phone to retrieve the message I hoped was there regarding my lost cell. I couldn't remember my damn voicemail password. When I listened later from home, I heard my own recording, "I can't remember my password!"

One of the gals in my class told me that the cops could help me. When she'd taught school, a student's phone was stolen, and the cops were able to track it to the home it was taken to. This would never have occurred to me. Here was another resource.

My adrenaline was pumping hard. I was on fire with the powerful intention to retrieve my phone. My plan of action was to go to the Apple store on Prince Street to see if someone turned it in. If it wasn't there, I would make a beeline to my local precinct uptown and enlist their help.

When class ended, I bolted out of the building like a bat out of hell. I saw a cop. Great! "Where's the local precinct?" I gushed. I could do the police thing now. Why not?

He had no idea. He wasn't NYPD. He was with The Fed (the Federal Reserve, which is not a governmental agency. Just so you know, the joint that controls the US money supply is a "private entity." Hmmm...)

"Okay. Where's the subway?"

He was of no use there, either. He was just protecting the dough and the criminals who control our "central bank" and manipulate our money supply. I kept running, trusting my radar to find a subway. I found the huge new Fulton Street Station with a zillion trains and never stopped moving. My eyes and brain kept recalculating my trajectory and destination as I looked at numerous signs. I jumped on an uptown express, my heart racing. It didn't go to Prince Street, so I had to jump off at Brooklyn Bridge and hop on a local. But before I did, I saw something very intriguing in my car. A young Japanese lady dressed all in pink with bunny rabbit shoes (You know what I'm talking about. These kids dress like stuffed animals. Her shoes had rabbit ears.) Anyway, she was like a little doll herself, perfect, pretty and...holding a red iPhone. I took it all in and understood what I was seeing. No, it wasn't my phone, but it was a sign. Two signs, actually. Follow the White (or pink) Rabbit, and follow the red iPhone. I smiled. Spirit gave me the heads up. I was on the right track.

I hopped off on Spring Street, trying to remember if the store was on Spring or Prince, but really, just continued to follow my body. It knew where to go, even if my mind was a bit fuzzy. Unlike empty Wall Street, there were *hordes* of people in Soho on a Saturday, and I wove through them like a guided missile. I dashed into the store. "Where's your lost and found? Did anyone turn in a red iPhone?" I blurted.

"We'll have to call downstairs."

I was still pumping with adrenaline. He called downstairs. Shook his head. Nothing. Another guy bent down under the counter and rummaged around. He reappeared a few seconds later holding my phone.

I screamed, "My phone!!!" I danced, I twirled, and then hugged several employees, one of whom did not appreciate the gesture. But Justin, who was wearing a plaid skirt, welcomed my enthusiasm. He was the one holding my phone. They needed to make sure I knew the security code. I passed the test. Mind you, did they notice the message on my phone saying, "This phone is lost, please call..."? If I hadn't picked up my phone in person, would they have bothered to follow up? I somehow doubt it.

Bottom line, I had the phone back in my hot little hands thirty minutes after I raced from Wall Street, two and a half hours after I lost it. My body knew where to go and what to do. It has its own wisdom. I was an iPhone-seeking missile. Was there logic involved in retrieving my phone? Yes. But there was also way more than logic at play. We are multi-dimensional and can benefit from that fact when we open up to the possibility of it.

During the one month that I knew my senior neighbor Shirley was leaving, I checked on her daily and helped her frequently. She snapped at me several times, once so harshly that I burst into tears after she hung up on me. In the past I might have shut her out, refusing to assist further if she was going to bite the hand that fed her. I thought about telling her how I felt. However she's pushing ninety, so were we really going to have a meaningful conversation, especially when she's so stressed and overwhelmed about her move? I was able to let it go, and it was obvious from her fawning behavior shortly after the fact that she knew she'd done me wrong. I accepted her wordless apology and was happy to continue helping her. These were my last days with her, after all, and we did have a close kinship over the decades.

I came to a realization. When my mother died, Shirley stepped to the fore and (in ancillary fashion) served as pseudo surrogate. She provided the adult forum I never had with my mom, listening to details of my work and love life, something my mother never had the chance to do. I had helped my mother in many ways, and was able to help Shirley, too (I was her handy-man and computer expert, among other things). Shirley listened to me, took me out on my birthday, and held my mail when I went away. So her departure signaled a rite of passage, even though I'm now a "big girl."

Despite her assiduously prepping for her move with daily lists and chores, when I checked on her the afternoon before the move, she was grossly unprepared. So, I stepped up. "What needs doing?" Whatever it was, I did it. She was exhausted, slumped over, and couldn't even look me in the face. The lunch out she had promised me days before never happened, nor did the dinner out she had offered. I told her it didn't matter, now was the time to pack and prepare. On our last night she couldn't even order food in. She was nauseous, and I didn't need a Last Supper with her. I was sending her off to summer camp for seniors.

I was up till one a.m. that night, packing, lifting, and organizing her personal effects after two consecutive days of strenuous gym workouts on my part. I was a zombie. But despite her constant insomnia, she was petrified of sleeping in on this most important of days. She had packed all her alarm clocks. I was up at six and called her, and was back helping her by seven.

When the mover arrived at nine, the guy beamed from ear to ear and said to Shirley, "You did all my work! I was supposed to pack for you! This'll be easy, thanks!"

I stared at him, dumbfounded. "*I* did all your work."

He got paid for my backbreaking labor. Shirley had left a few plates in the kitchen and a few garments hanging in the closet for them to pack, but had entirely misunderstood the terms of the moving agreement (and what she had paid for). They were to pack everything, *including* her dishes and garments. With the movers there, I was again "in her hair," and she made it clear my presence was not wanted. I went home and cried, not from being dismissed, I was used to that from her by now, but from sheer exhaustion and from finding out that what I had spent the last eighteen hours breaking my back doing was utterly unnecessary.

This put me in mind of an incident years ago, when my sister and I visited our grandmother in her nursing home. She was pretty frail, and so tiny the nurse called her Peanut. My grandmother was German, and so was her roommate, a tall, willowy woman who called me "schatze" and begged me while gripping my hand, "Bitte. Kaffee?" She wanted a cup of coffee with cream and sugar. I got it for her. The nurse yelled at her when she caught her with the contraband. For some stupid-ass reason, this simplest of pleasures (in a Styrofoam cup, no less) was denied a very old woman. Ridiculous.

My grandmother's dentures were out on the bathroom shelf. They were disgusting, covered with all sorts of muck. I bit the bullet, grabbed them, and scrubbed with toothbrush and toothpaste until they were...less disgusting. Very proud of my bravery, I emerged from the bathroom and told my sister what I had just done.

She replied, "What are you talking about? Nana's dentures are in her mouth."

I had just cleaned her roommate's teeth.

The feeling of dismay was about the same as with the movers.

Shirley left two notes written on paper towels. One was to the movers, *DO NOT REMOVE ROBE, HAMPER, OR SHOWER CURTAIN* (these were going to the Salvation Army, via me) and the other was to me, *VALERIE, WORDS CANNOT CONVEY MY ETERNAL GRATITUDE. I WILL CALL TONITE. SO M...*

Like Joseph of Arimathea's unfinished Aramaic message carved on the cave wall in *Monty Python and*

The Holy Grail, "Here may be found the last words of Joseph of Arimathea, 'He who is valiant and pure of spirit may find the Holy Grail in the castle of Aaaargh…!'"

I discerned the intended meaning of Shirley's last few letters. "So much love."

I don't regret packing Shirley's things. It was an intense night, and it represented our final hours together, with me helping her. I saved her life that night. She was in a "state," believing that she was utterly unprepared, and I prepared her. She wrote me after her move to say, *If you hadn't helped me that night, I'd still be sitting in my old chair.*

While looking for new housing for years, she didn't tell me of her plan to move until just a month prior. She shared her reason for moving to a home for independent living thusly—the building that we've lived in since the 1970s has changed vastly over the years. There are lots of young couples with babies, nannies, and maids galore. Then there are the old timers, some of who are in wheelchairs and walkers (I'm somewhere in between the two demographics.)

Shirley referenced someone who'd died in the building and said, "I don't want to leave the lobby on a stretcher."

My final gift to Shirley came in the form of words. I found her still in the lobby (after the movers packed her last teacup and blouse) waiting to be picked up by a relative and driven to her new home. I was just back from yet another workout I couldn't believe I had the strength for, but adrenaline was still pumping through me and I needed the release after all the stress with her. Shirley was drained of all energy, and she sat slumped on a bench by the front door.

She was sinking into a quicksand comprised of exhaustion, stress, and insomnia. Hunched over like a 9000-

year-old mummy, she still couldn't look at me. She looked only at the ground. The night before I had repeatedly commanded her to stand up straight and look me in the eye since she was withdrawing into herself like a traumatized person. I imitated her atrocious demeanor, hunched over, eyes down. Despite how spent she was, I reminded her that I was doing all the work, and when she snapped at me yet once more, I finally stood up to her. "Are you complaining?"

That shut her right up.

I looked at her seated in the lobby. "You remember what you said to me? You don't want to leave this lobby on a stretcher? Well, you're not. Stand up straight, chin up. You're *walking* out of this building."

Shirley bequeathed me a bag of frozen peas and a can of string beans. I also inherited her string, ribbon, and plastic and paper bag collections. She took her plastic bag ties (already twisted and used) with her for future use. My foyer is filled with twenty bags of her unwanted stuff awaiting the Salvation Army's pickup in a month.

Shirley is now up north, eating endless lox with the "walker brigade." It'll probably take her a year to unpack. Despite her virtual death, she called from her new haven, and we had a lovely chat. I've often felt abandoned when people moved, and wrote off the relationships. Hearing from Shirley was like hearing from a ghost. I enjoyed our ghostly conversation thoroughly. It was like she had never left.

I've had another realization about my relationship with Shirley since she "departed." After years of looking after my mother, and looking in on Shirley, I'm not "on call" anymore. I've no one to care for now but myself. And that's a good thing. I'm free.

I'm softening. This too, is a part of my mystic and spiritual opening. The Land of the Purple Glove, The Orange Earring, and The Red iPhone is an expansive place. Wonder abounds.

AFTERWORD

(More Signs, Symbols and Sigils)

Many things have been prophesied for me in the past. Things I didn't understand or care about at the time, as is often the case with psychic messages. For instance, twenty years ago (or thereabouts) I was told, "And someday you will write."

I couldn't have cared less. I wanted to be an actress. Writing was never my goal.

Son of a gun, The Divine Energies were right.

When seeking healing from doctors, alternative therapies, and healers, I also sought psychic and spiritual counsel to heal my physical maladies. I was told on more than one occasion that I had the ability to heal myself. That just pissed me off, 'cause if I knew how to, I would have.

I was also told that I was a channel. Uh huh. What do I do with that little tidbit? I go to channelers, read channelers, listen to other channelers. I'm a channel? For who?

Over the decades, I've been encouraged to meditate, write, automatic write, and channel. Recently, Nicole blurted out to me that I'm a medium. Now, you know from my writing that, even though I'm nurturing my expanding psychic and spiritual self, I still follow others who are channels, mediums, and psychics. Nothing wrong with that, right?

What was Nicole talking about, "I'm a medium"? On the other hand, I *do* see things not physically present, including geometric forms and visions of people on occasion, and I do see, hear, and "know" things, so who's to say *where* that information is coming from? Perhaps I am a medium after all. Sometimes it's hard to put a label on your own talents and abilities.

A few weeks after that message from Nicole, I went to hear channeler Rae Chandron speak at the United Nations. He's from India, but lives in Japan, and is a regular contributor to the monthly *Sedona Journal of Emergence*, to which I've subscribed for the past fifteen years (and highly recommend). Rae had sent me some customized sacred alphabet letters via email (per an offer in the journal) specifically divined for me. While I'm not a UN employee, I live nearby, and got permission from the organizer to attend his talk on symbols and numerology. During the course of the lecture, Rae asked who wanted to receive "their numbers." I raised my hand. Why not? He'd already given me my letters.

I was the first to stand in front of the crowded room and he intoned: "You are a psychic. You are a medium. You are a clear channel. Nostradamus is here with you. You have healing energy in your hands. You are going to have a full opening now."

Gee, a girl can't ask for a better introduction. He also drew my powerful sacred symbol (a geometric design) coupled with my numbers, on the black board. I was mesmerized by the image. No one else in the audience received anything like my message.

A week after that, Nicole noted, "Hmmmm…You

met someone. You were given a gift. You're going to be opening up big time with your abilities now." I had not told her about my encounter with Rae. She continued, "It's time for an upgrade. You're ready for it. But remember, *you* called him to you. He facilitated the opening, but it's your power, not his."

My most recent message from Nicole pertained to ownership (and use) of my abilities. Spirit upped the ante. Her guides said that I have to claim my power, that I must put it into practice. I have to admit, I have felt sheepish doing so, "Aw, gosh, I'm a *what*?" But yes, I am a Woman of Power and Vision, and I'm claiming it, growing it, developing it, using it, and now *you* know. I'm "out."

I'm a psychic, a medium, a clear channel, and I have healing energy in my hands.

A specialist in the absurd, I'm still doing crazy things like cracking a rib while diving into a trashcan. Let me explain. I found a beautiful white flower on the street late at night, and as I continued walking found another. Ahead of me, I spotted a young couple on the corner holding a gorgeous bouquet (pink peonies, green hydrangeas, and white lisianthus) from which the flowers I found had obviously fallen. As I approached, the guy tossed the massive bouquet into the trash, and the couple walked away.

I looked in. The can was empty so I had to reach *all* the way down to grab the bouquet. There were a few loose flowers at the bottom as well. I have a "no flower left behind" policy, so I reached and reached (and reached) down for that very last flower and cracked a rib (all right, so maybe it was just bruised, but it hurt like a mother for a week).

And then I discovered *why* the guy tossed the bouquet. It weighed about twenty pounds. I had a cracked rib and stronger biceps when I returned home with my stunning prize.

More wackiness ensued when I made super healthy (and tasty) organic ginger/orange/molasses whole grain cookie dough with ground flax, oat bran, and brown rice flour (among other things) that was so dense it nearly killed my industrial Kitchen Aid mixer. Now that's a healthy cookie! It stops machinery in its tracks. *Is it a cookie, or a hockey puck?* It's a cookie *and* a hockey puck!

I've been wading through stuff in my home and releasing items to be given to charity. In tabulating my massive shoe collection, I put some back in the closet, some in bags to be given away, and left some on the floor to be dealt with the next day. Psychic that I am, I awoke at four a.m. to the *very* soft sound of chewing. I listened, pondered, then turned on the light. It was my puppy, Milo, chewing on *the* most expensive pair of shoes I own. They're so expensive, I never wear them. I just look at them. I don't want to mess them up.

Having made progress in my personal growth, I removed the shoe from my puppy's mouth without screaming, scolding, or having a heart attack. I put the dog back in bed and put the shoe on my desk to assess the damage. My heart skipped a few beats, and my breath froze as I took it all in. Milo had *almost* chewed through one of the ankle straps, and had nibbled on the other one before deciding that the right shoe tasted better than the left. It was a vaguely traumatic moment, and, fully awake, I went back to bed feeling a bit like a disaster had just occurred. I also went to bed knowing that the *single* most important thing was that I had my amazing and beloved puppy back with me.

When I woke up, I hoped that the shoe was magically "healed" as a reward for my not freaking out. Nah. It was still messed up. I decided to have it fixed, and also decided it was time to wear the damn shoes. Expensive or not, what's your stuff for if not to use? Milo did me a favor. He broke them in for me.

Now, I have a favorite shoe repair store downtown (from when I used to work for JCrew corporate). From some Eastern European country, the guys are friendly, do good work, and are reasonably priced, unlike the repair joints in my neighborhood, which I've sworn off. It's cheaper to buy new shoes than to go to them.

A friend invited me to meet her downtown for lunch, so I grabbed the shoes to take with me for repair. While I waited for the bus, I eyed one of the local shoe repair shops I avoid. On a hunch, I walked in and asked how much for the strap. Now, I was prepared to pay up to $20 downtown. It was a good shoe, it needed good leather, and good workmanship. The young guy (not the nasty owner) running the shop uptown that morning said, "$10. But I don't have the right color leather." I was surprised by the low price, and figured he'd do a crappy job, so I took my shoe back. "Thanks, I'll think about it."

Downtown, my favorite place quoted me $26.00. For one lousy strap? I don't care how much the shoes cost, I'm not throwing good money after bad. As I walked out, I recalled that the last time I'd been there (a few months prior), they'd quoted me the same exact price to fix a pair of espadrilles. $26.00. I remembered the figure because it was so specific. Why not $25? That was a considerably bigger job, and I had decided against it because (with the repair guy's professional agreement) the shoes were just so badly made, it wasn't worth repairing them. I'd worn them *once* and the shoes fell apart (yeah, I'd been sitting on those babies for years, too, which is why they disintegrated, but at least they were cheap.) But what's with the $26.00? They can't charge that for *all* their jobs, can they? Was it something about my face? Was that their sucker price? Whatever it was, it rubbed me the wrong way, and now I'll never go *there* again.

I went back to my local joint in the afternoon. The same fellow who'd quoted me $10 was still there. We discussed the work that would be done, I paid him the $10.00 and he told me to return in twenty-four hours.

Well, surprise of surprises, he did a *kick ass* job on my shoe. You couldn't tell a puppy had ever been there. It was amazing. Magic. Good as new. He knew what had happened to the shoe, so he looked down at Milo and smiled warmly (and with humor) as he spoke to my pooch. *"Thank you."*

That experience was healing and eye-opening on many levels. One, I stayed calm, cool, and collected upon discovering the initial damage. Two, I'm finally wearing the nice shoes, which were made and bought to be worn, not stared at. Three, I learned that a good place can turn bad, and a bad place can turn good. There are lessons galore if you keep an open mind and heart. The world changes as you do.

My superintendent decided to stay on the job in my building for another six months. My other senior neighbor who moved with her cat to assisted living (due to her infirmities), now contends with the fact that Mr. Huffington (her cat) pulls the emergency cord (clearly a cat toy) in the middle of the night, bringing staff to her rescue.

More mystical madness. My Egyptian Temple cat Marlena is so soulful and spiritual that even her bowel movements have taken on profundity. She has taken to the tub as her toilet. She eschews the kitty litter, except for when the pine pellets are fresh, she'll christen the litter once with her pee, leaving it to her sister Celeste after that. However, as a general rule, Marlena pees directly down the bathtub drain, which is easy to clean (obviously). She poops *near* the drain. The patterns in which her poop lie are so intriguing (the pi symbol, for starters) that I've taken to calling them Crap Circles (a play on Crop Circles, for those who don't know). The patterns have been reminiscent of Stonehenge and the Sanskrit characters for Om. I'm not sure what the poop portends, but there's a message in there somewhere.

As regards the healing of my body, I'm doing it. Me healing me, that is. I know the body can achieve full healing (read Anita Moorjani's book, *Dying to be Me*). If I believe that someone else can do it for me, why *can't* I do it for myself, especially if I'm a healer? When it comes down to it, the few imbalances I'm redressing are best served by my own ministrations. I am claiming my healing power and authority and working my magic on me. I am healthier and stronger, more vital by the day. The proof is in the pudding.

The miracles are only just beginning. From retrieving my purple glove and red iPhone to summoning my dead dog Mimi back as Milo. Let's see what else I've got up my sleeve.

See what you can do, while you're at it. There is brilliance brewing within us all.

RESOURCES
(People and Places I love)

To schedule a guidance session with Valerie (healing, personal growth, psychic development, past-life regression) go to: http://valeriegilbert.weebly.com

My other websites:

http://ravingvioletvalerie.blogspot.com
https://www.facebook.com/RavingViolet/?fref=ts

Omega Institute, Rhinebeck, NY https://www.eomega.org

Kripalu, Lenox, MA https://kripalu.org

Esalen, http://www.esalen.org

Sedona Journal Of Emergence, https://sedonajournal.com

Esther Hicks and Abraham, channeling team extraordinaire. http://www.abraham-hicks.com/lawofattractionsource/index.php.

Nicole Gans Singer: http://www.teachingsofthemasters.org

HAPPY! The documentary. Brilliant. Informative. Important. http://www.thehappymovie.com

DON'T POSTPONE JOY!

About the Author

Valerie Gilbert is a psychic, medium, channeler, and healer. Born into an ardent metaphysical family, she is passionate about exploring the depths and heights of the Divine Mystical Human Experience. She shares this enthusiasm with others via her four books and blog, "Raving Violet," and through private and group sessions using guided meditation, intuition, psychic development exercises, personal growth dialogue, healing, and past-life regression.

An avid environmental, animal, human rights and peace activist, Gilbert is a native New Yorker and Harvard graduate. She lives in New York City and is a popular audio-book narrator on Audible.

www.ingramcontent.com/pod-product-compliance
Lightning Source LLC
Chambersburg PA
CBHW070054080526
44586CB00013B/1053